Acing Online Assessment

Get the skills you need to succeed!

Student Success books are essential guides for students of all levels. From how to think critically and write great essays to planning your dream career, the Student Success series helps you study smarter and get the best from your time at university.

Test yourself with practical tasks

YOUR PROGRESS

Diagnose your strengths and weaknesses

min   max

Dial up your skills for improved grades

Visit **sagepub.co.uk/study-skills** for free tips and resources for study success

STUDENT
SUCCESS

Acing Online Assessment

Your Guide to Success

Lucinda Becker
Felicity Becker
Anastasia Becker

Los Angeles | London | New Delhi
Singapore | Washington DC | Melbourne

Los Angeles | London | New Delhi
Singapore | Washington DC | Melbourne

SAGE Publications Ltd
1 Oliver's Yard
55 City Road
London EC1Y 1SP

SAGE Publications Inc.
2455 Teller Road
Thousand Oaks, California 91320

SAGE Publications India Pvt Ltd
B 1/I 1 Mohan Cooperative Industrial Area
Mathura Road
New Delhi 110 044

SAGE Publications Asia-Pacific Pte Ltd
3 Church Street
#10-04 Samsung Hub
Singapore 049483

Editor: Jai Seaman
Assistant editor: Charlotte Bush
Production editor: Sushant Nailwal
Copyeditor: Jane Fricker
Proofreader: Camille Bramall
Indexer: Authors
Marketing manager: Catherine Slinn
Cover design: Shaun Mercier
Typeset by C&M Digitals (P) Ltd, Chennai, India

Library of Congress Control Number: 2021940503

British Library Cataloguing in Publication data

A catalogue record for this book is available from
the British Library

ISBN 978-1-5297-7190-9
ISBN 978-1-5297-7189-3 (Pbk)
eISBN 978-1-5297-8770-2

Contents

Contents

List of tables

About the authors

Lucinda Becker is Professor of Pedagogy and an award-winning lecturer and tutor at the University of Reading. She has dedicated her professional life to creating independent learners who are confident in themselves intellectually, professionally and personally. Lucinda has written numerous study guides for students and works with undergraduates and postgraduates across the university. She is also a professional trainer and consultant, helping new graduates in engineering, science and law to become successful communicators and leaders. Lucinda is a Senior Fellow of the Higher Education Academy.

Anastasia Becker co-runs a private training company with a specialism in successful online assessment. She also teaches in both Further and Lifelong Education. Anastasia works as a Sign Integrated Performer using British Sign Language (BSL) within performances to add language and meaning for deaf and hearing audiences.

Felicity Becker has taught at the University of Reading and also runs a private training company along with Anastasia. She is currently working on her PhD. Within her teaching she is passionate about students recognising and applying their transferable skills in and beyond their university experience. She is the author of *Boost Your Employability* and co-author with Lucinda of *Seven Steps to a Successful Career.* Felicity is a Fellow of the Higher Education Academy.

All three authors are contributors to the SAGE online platform: Student Success.

To our Pa, who built the kitchen table on which we all work, and to all those who join us at that table.

1

Introduction

It is not surprising that many students find online assessment challenging. You are not on campus, and your friends are not around you as you face an assessment. For exams you might have to make your own judgements over timing, and for face-to-face assessment you are now face-to-screen-to-face. No wonder it can seem daunting. You can overcome most of these challenges with time and experience, but that could leave you at a disadvantage. Whilst you are getting used to being assessed online, you are missing out on the many benefits it offers. Getting to grips with online assessment means that you can minimise the challenges. So that is what this book is designed to achieve: helping you to feel comfortable with online assessment so that you can shine, taking advantage of the opportunities that we will share with you.

This book will guide you through every type of online assessment and, with many years of experience as educators in Further and Higher Education, we are in the best position to help you face these assessments with confidence. Online assessment looks likely to be here to stay, so, whether you are new to online assessment or more experienced, we will guide you along the road to success.

How to use this book

This book is designed to be dipped into as and when you come up to an assessment, but you might also like to look all the way through it first, to help you get your bearings. Each chapter focuses on a different form of online assessment and we have used a repetitive chapter structure to enable you to drop into the parts that are most relevant to you at any point. We recommend that you come back to this book prior to any online assessment challenge, to focus your mind and equip yourself for success.

It may seem that, with the move to online learning and assessment, you have even more work to manage with adapting to new systems, and this book should not be another thing on your to-do list but, instead, a guide to learning how to manage online assessments with aplomb. The book includes features that you will find beneficial:

- Top tips: key pieces of information and advice to help you along the way.
- Lecturer's view: gives you an insight as to what your lecturers might be thinking about online assessments or what they would like to share with you.
- Online hurdle: potential challenges with online assessment, preparing you to conquer them.
- Online benefit: a reminder to you as to why the online assessment is beneficial.
- Student quote: hear our students sharing their experiences of online assessments.

The work that you put into your understanding of online assessments now will pay off when it comes to completing these assessments for your course. Not only will it benefit you in an education setting but it also has longer-term benefits as you develop skills that are transferable to the workplace.

In this chapter, we will be looking at common anxieties around online assessment and solutions, how to tackle the assessment criteria, how to share effectively on screen, how we can all look good on camera, how to deal with off-campus assessments and, finally, how to handle technical difficulties.

Common anxieties around online assessment

By looking at the anxieties our students have shared with us about online assessment, and how we can overcome these, we hope to allay some of your fears.

> I am not very good with technology and am worried about getting a low grade because of that

You do not have to be a technical whizz to be able to complete online assessments, for two reasons: firstly, your lecturers are likely to demonstrate the platform that will be used for the assessments in advance (or a member of the study support team might do this) and, secondly, the educational platforms on which these assessments are most often held are user-friendly and have 'help' sections that you could access.

If you are feeling nervous about the technical aspects of the assessment, then getting help early on is a wise move. There are various ways to become familiar with the online systems you will be expected to use: browsing the system on your own, relying on the guides that your university has produced or asking a friend/study buddy/housemate to assist you. We have found that our students have created online groups through social media and so are able to share their thoughts with each other when they need a quick question answered or a bit of reassurance; this is particularly helpful for late-night or last-minute worries.

What if it looks different to what I have prepared for?

The first piece of advice we have for you is this: do not panic. When approaching an assessment, which can often feel stressful, it is helpful if it at least looks familiar but it is not a disaster if it looks different.

Top tip

> Being over-familiar can make us complacent and we can forget to read the assessment instructions carefully. If you are completely unfamiliar with an assessment format, remember that it could be useful to you, so take a breath and take your time.

Taking the time to carefully read what is asked of you will help you to take a moment to collect your thoughts and to focus well during the rest of the assessment.

What should I do if I cannot access the online assessment?

We are sure that everyone using online systems will, at some point, have encountered difficulties accessing something. As you might with any problem, try a varied approach to the issue. Firstly, contact the person/people listed as your first port of call for technical queries. Finding out who should be contacted if there is a problem is something that you should do before your assessments. Secondly, continue trying to resolve the issue yourself using your resources such as online help communities and how-to videos.

If you are given a long stretch of time to complete an assignment, such as a learning journal or project, then you should inform your lecturers if you cannot access the assessment so that they can send it to you whilst you work on getting technical support to access the online system.

Should I be looking at my notes?

If the assessment requires the use of class notes, textbooks or other learning materials, then that is fine. However, some of our students have told us that there is a temptation with online assessments to check their notes or other resources, even when not permitted. A grade is a reflection of your abilities, and it is important that it is an honest reflection for multiple reasons. Firstly, you will know at what level you are working and will be able to use this information to focus your studies and to improve. Secondly, your submission will help your lecturers to identify areas that need developing so that they can give you feedback and they may be able to tailor their teaching to support your learning. Thirdly, it is useful for your future employers to recognise where you might need support or further training. For example, if you are an English Literature student who has achieved a 2:1, employers might reasonably expect you to be able to write excellent reports. However, if you have achieved that grade through a lack of academic integrity, then they might be surprised to find you fall short of their expectations.

This, of course, will also be hugely stressful for you too in the long run, given the myriad systems in place to detect academic misconduct, let alone any innate belief you have about the need to be honest. Far better, then, to follow the assessment instructions and simply avoid the need to check your notes by revising thoroughly.

LECTURER'S VIEW

It is obvious to us when a student has looked back at their notes when they are not supposed to, and it invalidates the whole assessment even if they only did this for a small part of it. Far better to revise so well that you do not even need to consider checking your answers against your notes.

How do I prepare for an online assessment?

Your knowledge and skills

As with any assessment, your knowledge and skills are under scrutiny. Part of preparing yourself to respond to the assessment brief is to revise the subject in such a way that you are ready to complete the assessment to the best of your ability.

Preparing yourself to complete a particular assessment type is a skill that you will need to develop. For example, if you have never led an assessed seminar before, then you will have to begin thinking about the material you want to deliver and the resources that you might need or want to share, and then consider how you will run it online.

One way to get yourself ready for an online assessment is to think about how you would normally complete the assessment and then consider what may need adapting now that it will be online. For example, if you are used to writing notes on a scrap piece of paper, think about how this would work for an online assessment: you could, perhaps, have a Word document open to keep notes. If you usually look through all of the questions or answer them in a different order than they are laid out, think about whether that is still something you feel that you could do online. Also check this is still feasible online, as some assessment formats do not allow you to move back and forth between the questions.

Looking at a screen is a very different experience to looking at a hard copy of a document. Understanding how you work best with your device is a detail that is often overlooked and yet it is vital to doing well in your assessment because, by knowing how to manage your online assessment, you will be able to achieve at your highest level.

Getting feedback from a member of your household, a study buddy or your lecturer is a useful exercise in preparing for an assessment. If you are required to give a presentation or lead a seminar, you should practise this with an audience if you can, so that you get immediate and relevant feedback. If you do not have anyone to help you, you will find useful functions in presentation software that will allow you to time your presentation (slide by slide), get real-time feedback and to record it so that you can listen back to yourself.

Your workspace

Ensuring that your workspace is set up for your assessment needs to be done in advance and part of that process will be making sure that there is nothing that will disrupt or distract you.

student quote

'I wrote a list of things I needed to do before sitting an online assessment and pinned it up near my computer. It almost became my ritual, which calmed me down.'

You might like to use the following checklist to be sure that your workspace is ready for your assessments.

Preparing for my assessment checklist

✓ Desk/table is clear.

✓ Computer/laptop/tablet is set up with social media accounts/email/chats closed and any documents not relevant to my assessment closed.

✓ Note on the door telling my household I am undertaking an assessment.

✓ Phone and other devices on silent and put out of sight.

✓ Drink is nearby.

✓ The light in the room is not too bright or too dull.

✓ Logged into the assessment platform.

✓ Blank document (or 'sticky notes') open for notes or pen and paper ready.

✓ (If a tutor–student conversation/seminar/presentation or similar) Presentation or relevant documents/notes are open.

Technical preparedness

Be sure to log into the assessment platform with enough time to fix any technical problems that might crop up. You will obviously need to make sure that you have set up your login details before the assessment day and checked that you can get into the system. As we suggested earlier, knowing whom to get in touch with if there is a technical problem is a good idea. If you need any equipment such as a camera, headphones and so on, get them connected and ready with plenty of time to spare. If you are going to be using a camera, check that it is working by going to the camera app on your device and opening it to see what the background (and you against that background) look like.

How long should I take on my assessment?

The assessment brief will tell you how long your assessment should take. We have had students tell us that they feel that they should spend longer on an online than an on-campus assessment because it is open for a longer period of time. This extended accessibility is usually offered due to some students being in different time zones or having different work patterns. Do not be tempted to go on longer than the timeframe that has been suggested or mandated as you will not necessarily produce better work and it will prolong the stress you might be feeling.

Assessment times are calculated to give you enough time to complete the test and, if you take much longer, you are risking over-working the assessment. We prefer students to keep to the set time so that it is a true assessment of their abilities and is not marred by them second guessing themselves.

The mark weighting of the elements of an assessment is designed to help the assessors work out the balance of marks across the whole assessment. It is a useful thing for you to look at from the outset because it will guide you as to how much time and effort will be expected per question.

Top tip

If you are running out of time in the assessment, it is a good idea to summarise the key points that you would have written about if you had more time. The assessor may give you marks for the ideas even if you ran out of time.

How do I manage feedback and questions from peers and assessors online?

Here we are thinking about online assessed presentations, seminars and tutor–student conversations. Questions during an assessment, such as those you ask for at the end of a presentation, can feel a bit like an interview. You should be prepared to answer questions likely to come up but also have a stock response ready for questions that you cannot answer. People respond well to honesty and if you do not have an answer for the question asked, try not to prevaricate. If you need time to formulate your answer, take it by saying 'That is a really interesting question. Let me just think of the best way to answer you.'

Receiving feedback can be very useful to your development. However, not all feedback is valuable. If your assessor(s)/audience give you nice comments such as 'I learned so much' or 'That was great' then that is a lovely response. However, you will need more than that to improve and so you might choose to go back to them to ask for more details. Try to do this as soon as you can, as the further back in time the assessed event was, the harder it is for people to remember the details and give you specific feedback. You could ask, 'What was it that you found most interesting/useful?'

Is my assessment still private?

Yes, it is. The online systems used by your university will be extremely secure and your assessment will not be seen by more people just because it is online.

How do I work with others if we cannot meet in person?

Your university may have the online capability to have chat rooms and social gatherings virtually. Many of our students have commented that they have found social media groups to be invaluable when it comes to group work. There are some key things that you should do if you are working as part of an online group:

- Keep your communication clear. Take notes in meetings so that there is no confusion about tasks, dates and planned outcomes.
- Be specific. You should talk in detail about the individual tasks each member of the group will be doing so that nothing slips through the net.
- Set clear and fixed deadlines for each task. This will help to ensure the resulting piece of work is ready by the overall assessment deadline.
- Take responsibility and take ownership of your work. If someone is not pulling their weight and refuses to do so, make the lecturer aware, prior to the submission deadline, by being clear about which parts of the overall piece each of you has contributed.
- Meet regularly and be sure about who needs to meet and when. This will go some way to ensuring that everyone gets what they need from the group. Having everyone contributing to planning and review conversations will ensure that this remains a group project. Giving everyone the chance to speak can sometimes be a little tricky online so all of you will need to make the space for this, both in the time you allow and by encouraging everyone to use the online chat function.
- Be on time! It is especially difficult if someone is late to an online planning meeting as there is a social distance between everyone involved, potentially leading to awkwardness.

LECTURER'S
VIEW

It is clear when a group has not worked well together. You do not have to get on personally to be able to succeed as a group and this is a skill that will benefit you in your assessment, your future studies and the workplace.

Assessment criteria

You should have a look at the assessment criteria as early as you can so that you have it in mind when preparing your revision material, such as flash cards, posters, sample answers and so on. The criteria by which you will be assessed should be available from the beginning of your course, although your lecturer may only signpost you to it later on so as not to overwhelm you.

If you are uncertain about any of the criteria or how to meet them, talk with your academic tutor or lecturer. The feedback you were given on previous assignments might help you to pinpoint the criteria on which you need to focus, so take the time to look back at that.

The list of helpful terms in this book will illuminate the meaning of key words you might come across in assignment briefs, such as 'evaluate', 'analyse' and 'describe'.

Top tip

Check the assessment criteria weighting so that you know how much time you should spend on trying to meet each one.

Effective sharing on screen

Sharing a document or your desktop onscreen can feel like a challenge, but we have three simple points for you to consider when you are planning on sharing your screen.

1. What else will my audience see, alongside the screen I am sharing?
2. For how long will I be sharing my screen?
3. Can I share all the features of my document/clip?

Top tip

Look at your screen and surroundings as if you were a stranger attending a new classroom or a formal workplace. What looks too personal to share? Look at your physical surroundings as well as your screen and remove, hide or change anything that you do not want others seeing. Assessments that involve you speaking, such as presentations, vivas and seminars are likely to be recorded if they are part of a summative assessment. These recordings might be shared with an external examiner, so you will want to be sure that you do not have personal or private information on display.

When you are planning to share your screen to be able to show material to the others in the meeting, it is prudent to check what else they might see. Shut down your emails and any applications that might be showing that you do not want your audience to see.

It is good practice to consider for how long you want to share your screen. If you want to show something quite briefly, that should be fine. If you are sharing your screen to show several highly detailed files, then you might want to contemplate sending these in advance, so the other participants have time to digest the information.

Top tip

> Make copies of the assessment files that you have received or created on your device so that you have a back-up copy should anything go wrong. Just make sure that you change all copies if you change your master copy in any way.

By doing a test run of sharing your screen, you will be able to check that items such as audio from a clip or a hyperlink you are sharing still work when you share. We have found it to be quite a palaver at times to share every feature of a file with others in the meeting; by practising this you will ensure that everything runs smoothly and you will be able to manage the situation well.

Top tip

> Remember to switch the sharing function off when you have finished (in a similar way, get into the habit of lowering your digital hand in learning events). If you know that you always forget to do this, ask someone in the meeting to remind you. You will probably find that by delegating the task, you will remember to do it yourself!

If you are still feeling uncertain about delivering a presentation with a shared screen section, you can avoid this by sending the documents in advance and asking the participants to have the file to hand. Alternatively, ask a friend to help you work out the technical practicalities and practise in advance, or ask someone else to run the technical side during your assessment (if this is allowed within your assignment brief).

LECTURER'S VIEW

When you are delivering an assessed presentation (whether live or recorded), check your surroundings before you turn on your camera. Lecturers have seen it all: pets on laps, students in pyjamas, even the tail end of parties! We do not particularly object to pyjama-wearing students attending an online seminar, but we would like our students to recognise the formality of an assessment.

Many communication platforms offer a background blur or a simulated background. Although these are a super idea in theory, sometimes they can be a nightmare in reality. If you are wearing a similar colour to your real background, sometimes the computer makes you part of the background too! The flickering and changing of a simulated background can be a real distraction, particularly for those with a disability. You would be wiser to simply ensure that your actual background is inoffensive.

How to look good on screen

It is all too tempting when studying from home to throw on casual clothes and not bother to think about how you look. Assessors seeing this casual look will be influenced by it, no matter how impartial they try to be, so be aware of this.

The lighting will have an impact on how well you come across online. For example, if you have a bright light directly over your head (which is something that often happens in public spaces), your face will be partially shaded, and you can look washed out. If you have light coming from behind you, your face will be in shadow. This is problematic as people rely on your facial expressions for social cues and some people will read your lips to help them understand what you are saying, even if they are not hard of hearing. For the best results, try to find a place with natural light that is shining on your face.

Top tip

If you would naturally gesticulate whilst talking, check how this looks onscreen. You may need to find a way to limit this as it can be very distracting onscreen and can make you look chaotic, frantic and out of control.

If you are the host of a meeting and you need to record it, make sure that everyone is happy and aware that it will be recorded at the outset. This way, those who do not consent can have their cameras and microphones switched off. If you have practised and can manage a meeting as the host well, you will look competent and in control, which will set your assessor(s) and audience at ease.

ONLINE
BENEFIT

If you have a recorded copy of a presentation you have given, it is a clever idea to watch it back and identify the areas on which you need to work. This is great preparation for presentations in interviews and the workplace, as well as for future academic presentations you might be expected to give.

Managing online assessments

Managing your online assessments involves two key elements: your space and your mind. It is understandably difficult to study from home if the household is a busy one; it makes it even more important to prepare your space before you sit an assessment. You should remove all distractions – ensure that you will not be disturbed by people, animals or devices such as your phone or tablet. Allow yourself at least 15 minutes of quiet before you begin the assessment so that you have time to collect your thoughts and get into the right frame of mind.

ONLINE
HURDLE

There might not the same opportunity in an online assessment to carry out a post-mortem by talking it through with your peers. To overcome this, take 10 minutes of quiet reflection after the assessment so that you have the chance to recognise the aspects that did not go so well and the elements that did; this will allow you to walk away feeling content that you did your best.

Handling technical difficulties

If you come across a technical difficulty, do not worry. Staff at your university will be prepared for this to happen and, as mentioned earlier in this chapter, you should contact the relevant person/team about the issue as soon as possible. By informing them, you know that you are on your way to resolving the issue.

The best course of action to avoid technical difficulties is to check that everything is set up and ready well before the assessment. Check that your device has completed all the updates it requires, that your internet connection is strong enough to handle the online assessment and that you can access the site that you will be using.

Our final word...

A student who looks assessment-ready is one who we trust to do their best, so they are impressing us even before they begin the assessment.

Online assessments are an exciting prospect. They allow greater flexibility for you to undertake them almost anywhere, the online functionality increases your options, and you will have time and space to work at your highest level. There are, as with most systems, some hurdles to be navigated but, with this book in hand, we are sure you will approach them with confidence and determination.

2

Online assessed presentations

The purpose of an assessed online presentation is largely the same as for any presentation, but the feeling, and sometimes the marking criteria, can be very different, so that is what we will focus on in this chapter: helping you take control of the event and maximise your marks. We are thinking of an online presentation as you delivering a presentation on a platform such as Microsoft Teams, Zoom or your university's Virtual Learning Environment (VLE) (Blackboard or Moodle, for example). Your slides will be seen on screen, perhaps with just a voiceover or with you as a 'talking head' at the bottom or side of the screen. When we refer to a 'live presentation' in this chapter we are thinking of an in-person event in a room with a live audience.

LECTURER'S VIEW

Some students have told us that they would prefer to stand up in a room and present as normal, with their laptop positioned so that it captures them doing this. We tried it and found that our students' presentations tended to lose impact. It is surprisingly difficult to do well.

You might reasonably expect that an assessed presentation is designed to show off your knowledge, but in fact there is something else that is as important in this context, something that will frame all your preparations: timing. Having a mass of material for a dissertation is a great place to be, but for a presentation, it could be a disaster. The trick is to work out, early, exactly what you are being asked to do and to prepare precisely.

ONLINE BENEFIT

In a live, assessed presentation it is easy to worry so much about interruptions, or where you will stand, or exactly what you will say, that you overlook the obvious: this is you, telling a story. An online presentation is far easier in this way, because it relies on fewer factors: slides or other visual aids, and your talking head (or even just your voice).

What is an assessed presentation designed to show?

Skills

Four skill areas will be key to your success:

- Gathering the right material
- Creating an interesting story
- Preparing appealing visuals
- Engaging your audience

We will be covering all of these in this chapter, as the emphasis on each is different from a live event.

Your audience will probably consist of your fellow students, who will naturally be interested in your presentation if they, too, are being assessed this way. If your presentation is given just to a lecturer, you can also guarantee engagement as it is being marked, but you can aim for more than this. You can make sure that your audience really enjoys your presentation. There are two simple ways to achieve this – great visuals that help, and engage, your audience, and a story that is interesting.

Top tip

You will notice that we keep referring to your 'presentation story' in this chapter. That is because, regardless of your field of study, stringing together your information so that it follows a logical line that the audience can follow is the best way to present.

What is involved?

Try to avoid preparing material as if this were an essay. You are likely to show less material in a presentation than you would in an essay, because you are limited on time. You might still produce the same amount of material overall, but much of it might be in a handout. So, you need to plan really well, and this is where storyboarding can help you.

Telling your story

Storyboarding is a simple technique. Just produce a series of squares and insert in each square what you plan to include in that link in the chain that is your presentation. It helps to start this simply (just a few words or some bullet points in each square) and then work up your ideas (adding material, using symbols to show development, and including images to include in your presentation). As you go through, make sure that you are clear about which material you intend to include in your presentation, and which will be included in a handout.

ONLINE
BENEFIT

In a live presentation you have only two types of material: what you give during your presentation and what you offer in a handout. For an online presentation you have a third stash of material – the notes that you have beside you. These might include material to help you answer any questions, and a copy of your slides so that you can privately refer back to this material when you are answering questions or leading a discussion.

When you feel comfortable that you have the right flow of material, your storyboard squares have become your plan.

Table 2.1   Storyboard plan for a presentation

1. Intro topic and aims – climate change: what can we do to change our environmental impact?	2. What currently causes climate change? Visuals of waste, cutting down forests, fossil fuels, etc.	3. How do we, as individuals, create a carbon footprint in our day-to-day living? Images, possibly short clip.
4. What renewable energies and carbon footprint reducing technologies are in existence?	5. What does the future hold if we do change and if we do not change?	6. Conclusion – tips on how to reduce our carbon footprint and support a healthier planet. Visuals of a lush natural world.

Preparing visuals

In an online presentation your slides will fill the screen, so they become even more important than in a live presentation when you are standing in front of them.

Whatever your presentation topic, and however long you are given to present, always begin with the slide that gives at least your name and the title of your presentation (and perhaps the module name code, your student number and the date). Your marker (or the moderator or second marker) might not remember (or even know) your name, so this is vital information at the start. It also helps you to keep a clear record for yourself of this achievement.

It is impossible to say definitively how many slides you would need for any length of presentation. Preparing lots of slides can be reassuring, because it makes you feel that you have plenty of visual material to rely on when you present, but it could make problems for you if you are forced to gabble through too many slides. You will discover whether you have the best number of slides during your rehearsals. If you realise then that you have too many slides, you can identify slide material that can be moved across to your handout or your prompt sheet for answering questions, so it will not be lost.

When we prepare 20-minute online lectures for our students, we would tend to use about eight slides, plus an opening 'cover slide' with the title and perhaps a closing cover slide with an online link or similar. This might help to guide you – and remember that you might be given a set number of slides to use, so check on this before you begin to make your slides.

Producing slides for online assessed presentations is easier than creating them for live events. You do not have to worry about audience members being off to one side of the room or squinting at you because your font size is just a little too small, or (worst of all in a live event) sighing at you because they had a moment's distraction and you have moved on to the next slide. There are just a few pitfalls to avoid:

- Even online, slides need to have a larger font than you would usually see (minimum of 14-point font).
- Use a plain font such as Arial or Calibri so that your slides look clear and fresh.
- Consider including a slide that shows an overview of your presentation.
- Pictures and diagrams can be helpful, but only if your audience can read all the labels or other explanatory text.
- Do not be tempted to use features just because they are there – clever transitions between slides or creative layouts that move about can make your online audience feel seasick, as there is no distraction from the screen.
- Make sure you are clear on how the accessibility features, such as subtitles or captioning, work if you are expected to use these. Even if you are not using specific features such as these, make sure that your presentation slides help everyone in the group.
- Including animations can be effective or simply distracting – ask friends and supporters what they think at the rehearsal stage.
- It is easy, in an online assessed presentation, to click on a link that takes you and the audience to additional material such as an online clip. Make sure that this does not take up too much of your time, though, and make back-up material (such as additional slides you can go to) in case the link fails.

ONLINE
HURDLE

Online presentations can be unexpectedly difficult to finish. It is easy to panic when you reach your final slide and need to find the 'stop sharing' button. The best way to tackle this is to produce a final slide with 'Thank you for listening' and perhaps your name underneath as a reminder (and your email address if this would be useful). This slide gives you time to calmly keep control of the situation.

Engaging your audience

However well you present your slides, there is one truth about presentations that never changes regardless of whether the event is live or online: *you* are your best presentation aid and preparing yourself is the most important task ahead of you.

How is the online version different?

Students have told us time and again that the main difference is that it feels so different to be delivering an assessed presentation online as opposed to in a room full of fellow students and a lecturer. As one student told us: 'Just not having to be in a room with everyone else made it easier for me to present, because I just saw people's faces in little boxes on the screen.' This illustrates one of the reasons why, on the face of it, it might sound easier – and in many ways it is – but it can also feel a bit lonely and, somehow, more daunting because you will feel responsible for the online space in which you are presenting, and there are pitfalls and panics there that you have not faced before.

Although we are talking about your 'online space' as if it is a given, we know that this is not always simple. As much as possible, we would urge you to use the space and the tools that your university is providing – what they will be calling their Virtual Learning Environment (or VLE) – not because it is necessarily the best space, but because it will be supported by your university, so technical glitches can be fixed quickly.

Top tip

If you can avoid it, never pay for access to an online platform or online software. It is very rare that you cannot work with a 30-day free trial or set up a free educational account, and you need not pay for privacy if your university offers this to you as a matter of course. If you find that you have to pay for something, go straight to your seminar leader and your fellow students and find out where you can do the same things for free.

Even if you choose (or are required) to use the online space of your institution, you will still have options in a presentation. Unlike most other forms of assessment, you can use online software such as Prezi, Google Slides and Microsoft PowerPoint online, all of which (like many others) will help you to make an amazing presentation, so it is worth getting to know which software you prefer.

ONLINE
HURDLE

Things can go wrong on the day of the presentation, so even though you might plan to go online to access your slides on the day, make sure that you have a downloaded version offline, ready to go if needed.

What challenges will online presentations bring?

You will need to tackle the online tools, ideally well in advance (and remind your-self again nearer the time) so that you are not too stressed on the day. There are four basic functions you need to master:

- How to share your screen with others.
- How to keep a sense of the room whilst you present.
- How to use the chat function so that you can receive questions online.
- How to control the 'hand up' function so that you keep control.

LECTURER'S VIEW

When you are exploring the functions within your VLE or presentation software packages, remember that we might not be much more expert than our students in some aspects of the software. New software and VLE functions are being developed all the time, so you might find yourself on a shared learning journey with your lecturer.

Sharing your screen is easy enough to do: you will see an arrow within a square, usually, and this will be in one of the 'control panels' of the software – the same panel you might look at to turn on your microphone or camera, or to chat to others. There are just two common glitches that we tend to see. If you find that you cannot present because the arrow we have just described does not appear for you, it is very unlikely to be your fault. It is much more likely to be your lecturer forgetting to give you the correct permissions level. If you are not designated as a presenter for the session, you will not even see the right buttons to press. If you are able to share but nobody can hear you, or hear what you are trying to show on your screen, it is because you forgot to tick the 'share (computer/system/presenter) audio' when you set up shar-ing. This is easy to fix – just stop sharing and then try again, this time clicking that box.

Keeping a sense of the room can be very difficult when you are presenting. The chances are that you will see only the presentation slides, rather than yourself or anyone else, which means that it will not be easy to notice if anyone adds to the chat or raises a hand. This can be daunting but you will get used to it surprisingly quickly.

Our students tell us that they miss seeing us when they are presenting because they would usually look at us for visual clues such as a nodding head, a big smile or a meaningful glance at a watch or clock. If this is how you feel, ask your lecturer to interrupt you a few minutes before the end of your presentation to remind you of the time.

If you rehearse well, this sense of dissociation will feel more familiar to you, which helps, but there are also other ways to help yourself. You could tell your audience that you are stopping the presentation halfway through so as to check the chat function and to spot any raised hands. You could ask a friend to read the chat comments to you as you go along, so that you have only one disembodied but familiar voice interrupting you. Both of these can work well, but only if you allow time for it and you feel confident about controlling the situation once you are interrupted.

If you are being assessed on a timed presentation, it could work against you to allow interruptions whilst you are presenting, unless this is part of the brief you have been given. It is easy to lose track of how much time you have spent actually presenting if you keep fielding questions mid-event. You might find it easier simply to present and then deal with questions and comments at the end. It is a good idea to make sure, however you decide to run the presentation, that everyone knows the structure at the outset. Even if you are just following the brief, beginning with a reassuring sentence about when people can ask questions helps to settle everyone down before you present.

Top tip

You can be taken by surprise by how anxious you suddenly feel as soon as you are sharing your screen and all you can see are your slides. This can throw you off your game and, because it can happen unexpectedly, it might be a good idea to reassure yourself at the beginning by asking everyone if they can see and hear alright, and have a friend or the lecturer primed to answer you.

You will probably by now be familiar with using the chat and 'raised hand' functions within your online learning system, but they can become a bit of a nuisance when you are presenting. This is only because they could be distracting;

they are still a bonus for you when handled well. Tell people when you will be responding to raised hands (at the end, usually, unless part of your assignment remit is to encourage discussion throughout) and also when you will be looking at the chat.

ONLINE
HURDLE

Your presentation must keep to a strict time limit, but if you find that it takes some time to check that everything is working fine, make sure that you note down beside you the actual time you started to present, as opposed to the scheduled time you were given. That way, you need not become flustered over the timing.

Are there benefits to me with the online version?

Yes, undoubtedly. Once you have mastered the challenges we have explored in this chapter, you might find that you prefer to present online, for all the reasons we will outline here.

LECTURER'S
VIEW

If you decide that you prefer online presentations, you would not be alone. Although as lecturers we know that there are some forms of presentation that are better for the students in person, there are others where we are considering making the move to online presentations a permanent feature of our courses.

Here are some benefits that you can access through an online presentation:

- If your presentation is to be recorded, your seminar leader can just press 'record': no more hassle with setting up cameras. If you are anxious about presenting, this is a huge boon, because a camera right in front of you can easily put you off your stride.
- You will be giving your presentation in a very familiar space. You might have to clear people and objects out of the way so that you have uninterrupted time on screen, but presenting from your own room can be reassuring.

Top tip

> If you do not like the idea of presenting from your usual study space at home or university accommodation, ask whether recording rooms have been set aside for students on campus.

- If you think you might need to use some additional material, such as when you are answering questions, you can get the supporting websites up on your tabs bar before you present.
- If you want to point your audience towards extra materials, either those you have created or online sites, you can add links to these in the chat function at any point.

Top tip

> It can be tempting to add lots of links to the chat, and then find that you do not use them all, which could leave you looking disorganised. If you put all your potential links in a document, you can cut and paste them into the chat if, and when, you need them.

- You can rehearse with whomever you like, whenever and wherever you like. You will find that rehearsing with family and friends as an online audience is easy to arrange at any time.
- Group presentations will not involve endless messages to get everyone in a meeting each time you want to work together. Online material can easily be shared so that each member of the group can edit, and rehearsals can all take place online.
- Your audience have no idea what is around your computer. So, a drink and snack to keep you going just before you present, a sheet with the main points you need to make in large text beside you and a clock that you can see right in front of you are all aids that you can have to hand easily and without your audience knowing.

ONLINE
HURDLE

Even though nobody can see it, avoid a script. You might be looking at a script directly behind your camera, thinking that nobody will notice, but they will. Your voice will lack expression, you will be looking in slightly the wrong place, and you will be in danger of sounding bored.

- You might be able to record your presentation and simply play it to the audience before a live question and answer session. We have mixed feelings about this. Some students see it as a fantastic chance to divide their effort, producing the film and then giving all of their energy to the Q&A session. Others find it stressful, as they spend so long trying to produce the perfect film that their stress levels become unbearable.
- If you are using prompt cards (postcard-sized cards on which you write very brief prompt notes), you can add in coloured cards without the audience noticing. You might, for example, add in a coloured card that says 'halfway through' or 'smile' or 'click on the link in the chat now'.

Top tip

Your audience not being able to see your prompt material can be relaxing for you, but it does mean that audience members lose a visual clue. You can help here by using sentences such as 'So, to make my final point...' in place of the visual clue they would have had of seeing your prompt cards dwindling.

What do I need to know?

You will be given a brief (instructions and/or a rubric) for your presentation and we have noticed that the move to online assessment is bringing with it far more detailed and useful information online for students than they might have received in the past. The questions we are offering you here might be answered in the instructions you are given, or you might need to ask them directly of your seminar leader or lecturer.

- What is the title ... and is each student using the same title, or is yours unique, and how much leeway do you have to change the scope of the presentation?
- How long is it, and how is that time divided between the presentation and the Q&A or discussion session, if there is to be one?
- Do you get several attempts, if things do not go according to plan on the day?

ONLINE
BENEFIT

It would be most unusual for a student to be given the chance to try a live presentation more than once, but online events rely on technology that might glitch a bit on the day, or you might not be very familiar with the platform being used so you might be given the chance to have a second attempt, or be given extra time. It is worth knowing this in advance.

- How should you support your presentation? With slides, and/or a filmed demonstration, and/or links to online clips or resources?
- Is it a pre-recorded screencast or a live online presentation? If you are given the choice between giving a live presentation on screen and a pre-recorded presentation, think through the points we have made in this chapter before you decide.
- If it is a live online presentation, will it be recorded, and who will do the recording?

LECTURER'S
VIEW

In our experience even very nervous students forget the fact that they are being filmed online within a minute or two, because there is no reminder that it is happening. So, you only need to be asking this question to see if there is a recording that you could refer to later in your revision or to brush up your presentation skills for future events.

- Who will be in the room? There could be a marker (and perhaps a second marker) and perhaps your whole seminar group, but if the event is being recorded you might expect fewer people to be there for a live online event. Funnily enough, this does matter, so make sure you are ready for the right size of audience.
- What is the timeline? How long is the session overall? How many presentations are there in a row? Will there be a break? These details matter in an online event as much as in a live event: watching online presentations can be tiring.
- How do you share the handout, if there is one? This needs some thought. If you put it in a link that you reveal during the event, everyone can get to it easily and can cut and paste the link for future reference, but it might distract audience members as they see it for the first time. The best way might be to email it and set up a link, so that nobody misses it.

Top tip

Handouts are often dense and detailed documents, used as back-up for questions or for future reference, and not designed for detailed discussion during a presentation. In online events you can share a handout onscreen, which could be a simpler document that supports what you are trying to say whilst you show it onscreen. This would not replace your presentation slides, but can provide some useful support in a Q&A session.

- Will there be a timekeeper in the event so that someone will tell you if you have only a few minutes left?
- Do you have the choice of joining others to give a group presentation if that suits you better than an individual presentation?
- Will the chat material be available to you after the event?

This might seem obvious if you are used to using MS Teams, where you can go back to check the chat for some time after the event. However, your institution's VLE might have only a limited (or no) access to this function. If you lose the chat at the end of a session, you might ask a friend to cut and paste comments, links and queries for you before the end of the session.

- Will there be assessed presentations throughout the course or term, or just at the end?
- How much does the presentation count in the overall course or module mark?
- How much of the mark will be based on presentation skills, and how much on other factors such as preparation, materials and overall argument?

LECTURER'S VIEW

You will receive much more help from your lecturer if you are able to ask precise questions. Asking a lecturer to tell you a bit more about the presentation will usually get you a brief answer. If you explain that you have, say, six specific questions you will gain far more useful and relevant information and guidance.

Where do I go for help?

If you have a question about the assignment, it makes sense to ask the lecturer or seminar leader who set the task, but only once you have checked and double-checked the instructions you have been given. Bear in mind that basic instructions might be updated from time to time, especially if they are online, so keep checking back on anything about which you are unsure. If you are uncertain about one little detail and it is bothering you, or you are not entirely sure that you have understood something correctly, you might want to check with your fellow students before deciding whether to approach the lecturer.

You will also find online guidance on offer everywhere – and that is a danger as well as a help. You can spend far too long working through sites that help you create an amazing presentation with a particular suite of software, when your time would have been better spent using your more basic skills and focusing on the content of the presentation. Always make sure that you are getting exactly what you need online and then leave the site once you have enough information for now. You can easily bookmark the site for later use if you think it might be helpful.

ONLINE
BENEFIT

It would be unusual to find an online learning platform that does not have a chat function of some sort, and this can be a huge advantage to you when you need help with a presentation. Rather than worrying about asking your question on microphone, wondering if it is a silly question (it rarely is), you can just type it into the chat area during your next module session. That way the lecturer will see it and respond at the best moment.

How should I prepare?

Your preparation for an online presentation will be largely the same as for a live presentation, but you can be a little bit more creative in your rehearsal schedule, so we will focus on that here. For any assessed presentation we would recommend six rehearsals, but in the past most students would have rehearsed alone, maybe inviting a friend or two to watch one run-through. With our increased use of online contact, you have more options, so this is how we suggest you make the most of your rehearsals:

Rehearsal one

This rehearsal gives you the chance to make sure that the material you have fits into the time you have been given. You will be working from a set of prompt cards or even a script (although we would suggest that you move on after this rehearsal to presenting without a script, as it can make your presentation surprisingly lifeless on screen).

After this rehearsal, you will cut down or add to your material so that it fits the time you have. Remember to allow enough time to introduce slides that the audience will take time to ponder.

Rehearsal two

This is the last time that your timing will be the main focus of your rehearsal, and the rehearsal will not be difficult – you are just running through the material at a presentation speed, leaving time for your slides and other aids, to make sure that your timing works.

After this rehearsal you can work on your prompt cards, or prompt sheet, if you have them, to make sure that only the most important information is there, in bullet points.

Looking down at prompt cards or a prompt sheet right between you and the screen is very obvious in an online presentation. This need not be a major problem, but your presentation will look less forced if you use what is on the screen to prompt you or you have just one sheet with an overview of your presentation laid down to the right and forward of your screen, so that you can glance across to it. This looks more natural on screen.

Rehearsal three

In this rehearsal you are starting to get a good feel for the flow of your presentation and clear sense of the final timing.

After this rehearsal you will need to complete your presentation aids (both slides and any demonstration or links out to material) so that, from now on, they are included in your rehearsal.

Always have a back-up where you can. If the VLE or the internet is not working on the day you can do nothing about it, but if you plan to demonstrate something, make sure that you have filmed your demonstration in case it does not work properly during the event. If you are planning to show additional material online, take some screenshots of the most important parts of the material, if this is possible, in case the link fails in the moment.

Rehearsal four

Now is the time to invite your supporters to see your presentation. Luckily, they can be as many miles away as they like – this will be no barrier to them helping you. In this run-through you present as if on the day, asking your supporters to watch all the way through without interruption.

After this rehearsal you will be making decisions. You will change any aspect of the presentation that was pointed out to you as potentially problematic, as long as you agree with the comment. Although your supporters are in a good position to share with you how an audience will receive your presentation, you know the assessment criteria and your overall academic aim.

Beware of helpful interruptions that put you off your stride. You need to make sure that you get the timing right when you have an audience in front of you, so ask your supporters to put their comments in the chat area, if they like, but not to speak until you have finished.

Rehearsal five

This is your second, and final, full rehearsal in front of an audience of your supporters. You are not looking to make any changes, necessarily, but rather to boost your confidence and make sure that there are no little glitches you had missed in earlier rehearsals.

After this rehearsal you might be correcting typos, or redesigning a slide, but probably not much more than this.

You are going to need to think hard about whether you want your audience for this rehearsal to be the same as the audience for rehearsal four. If you are especially nervous, you might prefer to give your presentation first to family or a couple of good friends, and then move on in this rehearsal to sharing with fellow students. On the other hand, you might prefer the same audience for both rehearsals, so that audience members can respond in rehearsal five to the changes that they suggested in rehearsal four.

Rehearsal six

Now you are back by yourself. This is a run-through that you will do on the day itself, just to remind yourself of the flow of the presentation and to give yourself the confidence to deliver it in front of your online audience.

Make sure that all your links and any animations work on the day. You will have made some back-up, low-tech material so you can still go ahead even if there are glitches.

What should I do on the day?

- Ignore it for a while if your presentation is running later in the day – find something distracting to do so that your nerves do not overwhelm you.
- Rehearsal number six – your last-minute run-through – will help to boost your bravery.
- Have a drink and snacks ready so that your energy levels stay high.
- If you have friends standing by to ask useful questions in the chat, or to interrupt you if there is a technical glitch, remind them of their role.

- Once it is done, note down what you think was good and where you need to improve for future presentations.
- Transfer any notes you made during the event into a more permanent place for future reference.
- Ask a person you trust how it went – if you feel you have to – but then ignore it and get on with your day.
- If you have access to the recording, try not to watch and re-watch, but store it for later viewing.

How do I get higher marks?

An online presentation will be marked on the same basis as a live presentation, with the possible exception that the percentage share of available marks usually allocated to assessing your presenting skills might be reduced to take into account the fact that this is a less familiar environment for many students. Although there are similarities, do not overlook some aspects of online presentations that can work to your advantage:

- Instructions: you will always need to follow instructions precisely when you are presenting, but this is even more important online, when an early interruption if you have something slightly wrong can throw you off course.
- Slow down: you will always be talking at a relatively slow pace when you give a presentation, but online you can create a greater impact (and so potentially pick up marks) if you slow the pace even more. During your later rehearsals, ask your audience whether you are speaking at the right speed or whether you need to slow down a little.
- Timing: a live presentation usually requires you to prepare around 18 minutes' worth of material for a 20-minute presentation. This is because, although you might not expect it, presentations tend to run slightly slower than rehearsals. In an online presentation this effect tends to be exacerbated: you will allow lots of time to show each slide or link because you cannot be certain that everyone will grasp the material quickly, and you cannot always see them. For this reason, we would recommend no more than 17 minutes of material for a 20-minute presentation.
- Smile: if things go well, smile about it. More importantly, if things go a little wrong, smile about it. A smile shows that you are in control, engaged with your material and eager to share it with your audience. A little note beside your screen with the word 'SMILE' on it can really help you here.
- Keep to time, absolutely without fail: a nervous audience, and an anxious marker, worrying about when you are going to stop, will always work against you.
- Have back-up: make sure you have a little extra material to hand, open in a document or an online tab, so that you are ready to refer to it or share it if it is needed at any point.
- Control what you can control, and let the rest go: if the internet is playing up, or there is a glitch on your university's VLE, or a link breaks, or your demonstration clip fails to load, you will not be marked down. If you manage to deal with it with confidence and determination, you could gain marks.

What do students think?

Student quote

'It went by in a blur – I can hardly remember what I said.'

It is amazing how often your nervousness can seem to wipe your memory. This is why it can be useful to record your online presentation or ask a fellow student for some brief and constructive feedback straight after the event. You have prepared well, and you will have given a good account of yourself and your topic, so now is a good time to reflect on your skills.

Student quote

'I thought it would go slower. I got to the end with time to spare'

Adrenaline can make you speed up more than you would ever expect and this is rarely a problem. You will have rehearsed to a little under the time allowed and you will have been practising speaking at a good presentation pace, but do not be disappointed if you did not keep speaking right to the last moment allowed: this will be a good outcome, as nobody will be getting nervous about you going over the time.

Student quote

'I wish I could do it all again!'

Great – you have enjoyed using your new presentation skills and you will have plenty of opportunity to use them again in future. Whether online or on campus, the advice in this chapter will be there to support you.

Moving ahead

Reflecting on your experience

The primary retrospect benefit of an online presentation, compared to a live presentation, is that you can record it if you like – either through the platform on which you are presenting or through software on your own computer. This allows you to take some time to get a good perspective on how you feel it went. You could make some immediate notes later on in the day of the presentation, for example, and then give yourself time before you reflect back by watching the recording of the event.

LECTURER'S VIEW

We find it useful to have a recording of a presentation if a student wants detailed feedback on how they did and how they could improve, so if you think this might be you, try to ensure that a recording of the event is made.

Moving ahead in your studies

It is best to avoid simply watching yourself on screen and letting your emotions take over. You might cringe to see that you have a nervous habit when you present – the chances are that nobody else noticed it. So, rather than focusing on minor problems, think ahead and plan what you want to improve in your presentation style.

Top tip

Try not to overburden yourself. Three clear points for improvement are quite enough after any presentation.

Looking further ahead – how does this help professional development?

Professional presentations are likely to become part of your life even before you leave university, as you may well have to give a job interview presentation. Of all the online assessments you are going to learn to ace, this is the one that will be of greatest immediate value, so all the hard work you are putting in now will be bound to pay off for you!

3

Online assessed student seminars

Student seminars provide a platform for students to showcase their academic and practical skills in a way that a presentation alone cannot. A student seminar routinely requires not only a short presentation of the topic material but also asks the student to raise thinking points, create material such as handouts and to lead discussions and activities in a way that develops other students' learning. Having a breadth of skills being assessed may feel daunting but actually it gives a student more opportunities to gain marks.

Typically, a student-led seminar is split into three parts: firstly, a presentation or a showcase of the topic; secondly, student discussions or activities; and thirdly, a summing up of what has been learned and where to look further for more information. Be careful to manage the timings for these three sections to stop one of two things from happening: either leaving huge silences or reiterating the same information, or running out of time and having to stop discussions before they have achieved their outcome.

LECTURER'S VIEW

Student-led seminars are a useful way for us to assess whether the student does the preparation, understands the topic and can create material that is relevant; we know that students get nervous, but notice that this usually disappears as soon as they start talking about their topic.

What is an assessed student seminar designed to show?

Skills

Student seminars are an opportunity for students to showcase a number of skills including:

- Time management
- Research and preparation
- Sourcing and creating materials
- Raising discussion points
- Managing activities and discussions

We will be covering these key points throughout this chapter with particular emphasis on how to lead an online seminar, although many of the initial stages are the same as preparing for a live seminar.

Knowledge

Knowledge is key to creating a useful and interesting seminar. It is important to find out early on the purpose of being assessed in this way, either through a conversation with your lecturer or by looking in the module or course handbook. Look at the marking criteria and you will gain a better understanding of what you will be expected to include in your seminar.

Knowledge of the technology you are being expected to use is also vital in creating an inclusive and informative online seminar. You may need to arrange a meeting with your lecturer or IT or technical support to learn how to use the platform on which you are expected to run the seminar. They might also be able to give you some ideas on where to find online resources and material you can use. Ask a friend to join you on the platform so you can practise using all the functions prior to your seminar. Some platforms use breakout rooms, others have automatic captions and transcript software, others lend themselves to screen sharing. Regardless, all of these platforms will have slightly different ways in which they function and knowing how to use the software is paramount for a smooth seminar.

Once you know how you are being assessed and what time you have been allotted you can begin the creation process. A fruitful starting point might be to pinpoint what it is that you want the other students to take away from the seminar; this can lead to you creating two or three key questions you want them to consider in their group discussions or activities. Working out these points allows you to start putting your knowledge and research skills into action to create a short presentation. Make sure that the information you are providing for your fellow students is not so dense that they cannot digest everything but also is not so obvious that they find it tedious. The way to find a happy medium is to utilise your handouts: you can put links to further information on a handout and keep your presentation concise, conveying the main points. You are likely to be using slides and this can be particularly effective when presenting online as you can include links to videos or images that support the students' learning. It is worth checking that all your links work just prior to your seminar as material can be removed from online in the interim between you creating your seminar and presenting it.

Top tip

It may be prudent to have all your links lined up and open on your tab bar, although, crucially, paused and muted, so you can instantly find them and do not have to wait for them to load.

Engagement

LECTURER'S VIEW

When we are assessing student-led seminars we are looking not only at how our students have engaged with the material but also how they assist other students' learning. A good seminar should be interesting and informative. Remember this is not a lecture but a learning discussion.

By creating a seminar, you will naturally engage with the material you are research-ing and collating. In creating discussion points and activities you are considering how the other students will be engaging with the material. You will need to consider how you would like to engage across an online platform as this is somewhat dif-ferent to a live classroom setting. There are several methods to communicate online including using the chat function, screen sharing a presentation, using a whiteboard or annotation function, creating polls and inserting short clips.

You want to ensure that your material and your seminar are as engaging as possible as then students will want to join in discussions and activities, conse-quently there is less pressure for you to 'fill the gaps'. Your seminar will be more engaging if you include visual aspects such as pictures or short video clips and not too much dense text. This is why it is so important to make sure that, although you will have researched widely and have plenty of knowledge about your subject, you do not try to fit it all into your seminar. Pick out the key points that are vital for your peers to know about the topic and that will create discussion, and then signpost them to further information should they wish to learn more.

Sharing

Being able to share – your screen, audio files, links and clips, whiteboards and polls – is going to enliven your seminar and could become an important part of what you are trying to achieve. A seminar poll, for example, could give you original research material about the response to material, research that you might want to employ later in a module or course project.

ONLINE
HURDLE

Seminars are designed to create discussion, but this can be difficult to manage online. There can be a delay in hearing what someone is saying, and it becomes difficult if people speak over each other; you will need to manage this by putting in place a turn-taking rule at the start of the session, this may be by asking people to raise their hands, either in real life or virtually.

You may also need to repeat a summary of contributions to ensure that everyone has heard and understood. To do this well you need to verbalise a short summary of what they have said or incorporate their question into your answer. For example, if the question is 'When was Hamlet originally performed?' you might respond with 'Hamlet was originally per-formed in 1600'.

A positive aspect of leading a seminar online is that you can ask students to use online whiteboards or to go away and research or create a document of their ideas and share this across an online platform such as Google Classroom, Blackboard or Microsoft Teams. These documents are records of learning and can be accessed by all the students, meaning that far more information can be covered during the class and shared afterwards. This may be a useful store of information should you or any of your peers wish to revisit the information at a later date. You can also share your handouts online rather than having to worry about photocopying enough handouts for the session.

What is involved?

When creating a seminar, the task can be broken down into five sections: preparing material, preparing to present, preparing yourself, preparing discussion points and activities, and considering time management and how to lead activities and discussions.

Preparing material

You will need to be clear on the parameters of the assignment and then you can start thinking about researching the topic and creating material. As this will be shared online it can be useful to set up a Word document or use OneDrive with your key points as headings and then, when you find information, you can put it under the headings. In this way you can make sure you have a clear path through the seminar. Once you feel you have enough information under each heading you can then highlight it with different colours to indicate what you might put into the presentation, what might be on a handout and what is information you cannot use for this project but might be useful for a future assignment or even your reflective essay.

Top tip

Do make sure that you record where you found all your information for your bibliography, and it might also be useful for signposting your peers to further research after the seminar.

Preparing to present

This is where you will make your slide presentation, handouts and collate your clips. Slides can be a really useful resource for laying out your ideas but make sure you do not crowd them with so much information that you end up just reading them. The points on the slides should be a guide to remind you what you want to discuss and as a reminder for students when they look back at it at a later date. You can include links in here as well as visual resources. A benefit of leading a seminar online is that you can instantly share your screen to show videos or resources.

ONLINE
HURDLE

Be mindful that videos can sometimes be blurry or freeze when screen sharing depending on the WiFi strength available to everyone. If this is the case, then you can copy and paste the link into the chat box and the students can go to the clip themselves.

Preparing yourself

Once you have your material created and you know what you want to present, then it is worth talking through your presentation as a rehearsal. This can be by yourself, to check the timings, or to a friend or friends to gain feedback. This feedback can be particularly useful as, although you will be an expert on your topic, your friends are unlikely to be experts and therefore will be able to indicate where they got lost or where they needed you to explain something further. You will find that these rehearsals will also help you gain confidence in presenting. It is very different speaking about a topic than simply writing about it and these rehearsals will help you to resolve any issues. Please refer to the rehearsal process laid out in Chapter 2 of this book.

Preparing discussion points and activities

Once you have the presentation aspect completed you can work on the activities or discussion points. Ideally you will have already thought about what these might entail as you have gone through the research process but now is the time to work out what you would like the students to gain from this portion of the seminar. Sometimes a question or statement can be enough to spark a lively discussion, but you might also want to have a visual stimulus such as a picture or short clip. Equally, you might want the students to carry out an activity such as a quiz or poll or use the whiteboard function to create a picture of what has been described in a piece of text. Take a Jane Austen novel as an example: look at the descriptive language when setting the scene. The whiteboard can be used by all the students to draw what is described. In this way you can show how effective imagery is in a text.

Considering time management and how to lead activities and discussions

Before you create anything, you need to know how much time you have and break this down into presentation and activities. Next you can tailor your activities to ensure you have enough time for the activity to be completed and, crucially, for there to be feedback. There is little point in running an activity if there is not time to discuss the learning point afterwards to help embed the learning.

You will also need to allow time for questions and answers at the end of the session, or throughout if you would prefer this. The benefit of leading a seminar online is that you can ask people to put their questions in the chat function throughout the seminar, giving you an idea of how long you will need to answer them at the end of the session. There is something rather daunting about leading a live seminar and having no idea what questions might come up at the end of the session or, even worse, not knowing if there will be any questions but still having left five minutes that then are filled with an awkward silence.

Top tip

A good way to respond if there are no questions is to end with a final sentence such as 'Well, it looks like we have managed to cover all the questions during the session but if there are any questions that occur to you later on then please do get in touch or take a look at the handout for signposting to further sources of information'.

How is the online version different?

When leading a seminar online you need to make sure that you are comfortable with the platform on which you will be leading the seminar; these might include Zoom, Teams or your university's Virtual Learning Environment (VLE) such as Blackboard or Moodle. Most of these platforms include a chat function and breakout rooms, which can be useful for the discussion/activity part of the session. You might want to ask a friend to manage the technology as you run the session so that your supporter can find suitable moments to indicate to you that there is a relevant comment or question in the chat box. The main difference between leading an online session and a live one is time management. You will have to consider how to manage student contributions as well as allowing time to move between screen sharing, breakout rooms and sharing clips. These transitions usually take a little more time than in a live session where you can easily redirect everyone's focus back on to you.

When considering how to share online material it is worth noting that when you are sharing your screen you can become a 'talking head' in the corner of the screen so people will find it harder to see you should you wish to demonstrate something. However, this can also be a positive thing as it can be less disconcerting if you don't feel that everyone is staring at you. It is worth practising how you share your information prior to the seminar as you may find that to share a video, for example, requires you to click a box to share audio as well as video and, if you do not click this box, you will find you have no sound. You can also test whether you can be heard over a video or audio file as you may wish to comment whilst the video is playing.

Be aware that some people may find watching a 'talking head' difficult if they require lip-reading to access your seminar. Some students may also need a larger font or specific colours to access the text you are sharing. All of this can be easily managed but it is something you should clarify with your lecturer prior to your seminar. If lip-reading is required or you need the students to see you whilst you present, then you can instruct them in how to change their viewing mode or how to enlarge your video box to take up half the screen. This is something you can get assistance with, either by researching how online or by asking your lecturer or IT support for a tutorial on how to use the various functions of the platform you will be using. Make sure you leave time to instruct your peers in how to optimise their view of you and your material at the start of the seminar. You can also include information on how to access the chat function, use the emoji responses and 'pin' you if they wish.

ONLINE
HURDLE

Access needs should be met and are somewhat different from classroom settings. You may need to consider how the platform supports a range of needs, such as being able to enlarge documents, view an interpreter or block out background noise. Check this prior to your seminar.

Conversations can feel more stilted online if they are not handled well. A way to allow conversation to flow is to establish early on that the students can write their questions or comments in the chat function and that they can raise their hand, virtually or actually, to get your attention should they wish to comment or ask a question at a specific moment. In this way you may find that students who would not feel comfortable speaking in front of the group may be more vocal through the chat function.

Due to the online nature of the seminar, you may find that you need to adjust your expectations of timing. This is something that we have already discussed in this chapter but is worth noting again here. Make sure you practise your seminar, giving slightly more time to group or pair work to allow for the technological delays.

Online seminars lend themselves to breakout rooms and discussions but are possibly less suited for practical activities. Your first port of call is to pinpoint what you want to achieve from the activity or discussion part of the seminar and then explore the online options such as quizzes, creating online play readings of an excerpt or passing a story around the group. There are plenty of ideas if you search online for fun activities that can be done by a group over the internet so it is worth having a think about what might engage your group.

ONLINE BENEFIT

If yours is the only student seminar in which these creative options are being used, you will instantly stand out from everyone else. The marker will be impressed and will remember you in future as a student who took the trouble to produce interesting and engaging material.

What challenges might an online student seminar bring?

If you are leading a seminar as a group, then you need to discover how to co-host. This is usually possible between two people on most online platforms, but you do not need to be a co-host to be able to assist in the group. You can also divide up the responsibilities as follows: one person is sharing and moving through the slides, one person presents, one person watches the chat and makes sure that any relevant information or questions are being included at an appropriate time.

Preparing for a group seminar online can be challenging on a practical level, just finding time for you all to meet and prepare materials. It is much easier to meet online and there is also the ability to record a meeting should someone not be able to attend, so they can catch up at a later date. Planning early is vital to ensure you all have the time you need to prepare your parts and to ensure you are all suitably confident in the seminar material before you have to lead it. There are times when there is an unavoidable incident leading to a member of the team not being able to present; in this case it is important that someone can take over and share this material, so take the time to understand each other's sections in case you have to present them. You will find that this also allows you to support each other in activities and group discussions. You will all possess different levels of technical skills so be kind to each other and be willing to learn from each other.

It is very clear when a group has worked well together, and you can see this particularly in how they divide up the tasks within the seminar. It is lovely to see a group coming together to cover a missing peer, ensuring that the seminar continues in a positive, cohesive way.

Rehearsing online will help build your confidence and this will be obvious to your assessor and your fellow students. You may need to persuade your friends to help in your rehearsals so they can let you know what is and is not working through the technology.

One of the surprising things about working online is that quite often people do not turn on their cameras, leaving you presenting to a blank screen. This can be quite disconcerting initially as you do not know if the students are engaged. The benefit to presenting to a blank screen is that it can feel like a rehearsal and reduce anxiety. So, how do you check that people are engaged and understanding? Again, the chat function can be useful here and so too is getting everyone involved in breakout rooms or in a task. This allows you to check that they have understood what you have presented as well as helping them to further develop their learning.

Are there benefits to me with the online version?

There are several benefits to leading an online seminar, one of which is that you will be in a familiar place and therefore will be able to set up your space entirely as you wish. All your links and paperwork will be exactly where they were in your rehearsals. Another benefit is that it might be recorded and there is no need to set up a camera as it can all be done automatically; this is particularly useful if you wish to look back at what happened for a reflective assignment or to talk about what was discussed or consider areas for improvement.

A useful aspect of presenting online is that you can surreptitiously write or type notes of things you want to feed back into the discussion at a later point or things you want to remember for a future project or for reflection after the seminar. Be aware that people can still see you even if you are screen sharing and therefore will be able to see if you are looking disinterested or madly writing notes.

Sharing your handouts online can be done easily in advance or after the seminar without worrying about getting to a photocopier. You can also leave space in your presentation to add students' comments, developing your initial presentation into a working document that can be shared with everyone after the seminar.

The point of a seminar is to share ideas, opinions and facts, to raise questions and to make connections, and an online platform can be beautifully designed for this interaction if used appropriately. You can use a group whiteboard that can then be saved and shared, fellow students can put links they have found into the chat box, sharing their knowledge in an immediately accessible way, and everyone can jot down their ideas, collectively or individually, in a document for later use. Occasionally seminars can be recorded and shared with students who have missed the original version, allowing students to catch up with their peers in a way a live seminar cannot provide.

What do I need to know?

Initially you need to find out what the seminar is about and what percentage of the seminar time is expected to be presentation and what percentage is expected to be discussion and/or activities. Once you know how long it is you can start thinking about how you want to support your seminar, for example, through sharing clips, slides and activities such as quizzes. Another consideration is knowing what you are being marked on. Take the time to look at the marking criteria and clarify these with your lecturer if you are unclear on anything. If this is a group-led seminar then you need to know what you will have to submit to prove that you were part of the creative process.

On a practical level you will need to know whether the seminar is being recorded, who will be 'in the room', what platform you are expected to present on and how this will be set up. As in a viva or professional discussion, you might find there is a second marker, moderator or other academic in the room. Knowing who will be there in advance can help you to feel confident when entering the room. Most learning institutions have a VLE where you can share your handouts before or after the seminar. Find out whether you are expected to write a reflective assignment after your seminar and what the deadline is for this. Keeping the information from the chat box can be useful for reminding you what happened during the seminar, and you might find it useful when writing your reflective piece, so either copy and paste it before closing the session or find out whether it will stay in the link after the event has finished so you can revisit it later.

Where do I go for help?

If you need help accessing the platform and its functions, then first and foremost you should contact your lecturer or academic support staff. It might be that the IT support department has created online tutorials showing how to utilise various online platforms effectively and these can be beneficial to watch prior to creating your seminar to give you ideas on how to create interactive seminars.

Top tip

There is a plethora of online help and advice when using an online platform to present. It is worth exploring these but try not to get caught up with learning all about the platform to the detriment of your seminar planning.

It is likely that if you are giving a seminar then your peers from the same module are also about to give a seminar, so utilise the student body to help you generate activity ideas or to rehearse with you, as you can reciprocate. The online world can be a great place to collaborate and support each other.

How should I prepare?

Prepare for your seminar as usual, but with the added factor of online. This is an exciting time to explore how you can use technology in a fun and creative way to produce engaging material and lively discussion. Make sure you rehearse online, preferably with a friend who can tell you if they cannot see or hear your screen share. As delightful as technology can be, do make a back-up plan that requires less technology in case a clip does not play or your slideshow freezes. Always have a printout of your notes, slides and handouts next to you just in case the technology does not work.

What should I do on the day?

If the seminar is later in the day, then do a run-through in the morning if you would like, checking that all your links still work, then it is best to try to ignore it until half an hour before. Any last-minute changes or additions can create confusion during the seminar.

Half an hour prior to the seminar, log on to your computer and make sure you have your presentation and materials set up. Check that your environment is set up too: this may involve making sure there is a bottle of water to hand, that the room is well lit and that there is nothing distracting behind you. You can also quickly review your lesson plan as a reminder of the order. Try not to log in to the class until a few minutes before starting otherwise you will sit there becoming more anxious.

Top tip

Remember, you can always enter the 'room' with your camera and microphone turned off until you are ready to start.

Once you have finished the seminar take a few minutes to note down what went well and what areas you need to improve on for future seminars. You might find this reflection time will also help you internalise what other students contributed to the seminar. It can be useful to receive constructive peer feedback.

These notes might feed into your reflective piece of work if this is required by your lecturer. If you lead the seminar as part of a group, it might be worth staying online whilst everyone else leaves so that you and your group can discuss then and there what went well and what could have gone better. Make sure you copy and paste anything from the chat box as this might be a useful reminder when writing up your experience.

Ask a person you trust how it went – if you feel you want to – but then ignore it until you come to write your reflective piece; a day away from it can settle it better in your mind so instead of focusing on the one time you mispronounced a word you can have a clearer perspective of how the seminar went overall.

If you have access to a recording of the seminar, try not to watch and re-watch it. A recording can be useful if you particularly want to quote someone or need to clarify a point. Quite often the anxiety of the moment can leave blank spots in your memory so a recording can be useful to help recollect key moments.

How do I get higher marks?

Follow the instructions minutely; this is always a good idea, but especially important in this context. Check with your lecturer if you are unsure about anything and ask to be shown how to use any software if it is something you have been asked to use. Recording this demonstration is a good idea. Make sure you make these initial checks with your lecturer early on so that you have plenty of time to create your seminar and to avoid going down one path only to realise that you misunderstood the assignment.

Do not overstretch yourself just because you have access to everything online. It is better to lead a technically simple seminar with really good content rather than making a technically complex seminar with no depth. This is equally valid when considering your topic; you may find masses of interesting information and want to share it, but you could end up with too much to fit comfortably into the seminar. The way around this issue is by utilising handouts that can signpost students to further sources of information should they want to find out more. Your research does not need to go to waste as you can include it in your presentation notes or reflective essay when handing it in to your lecturer to show that you have a breadth and depth of knowledge and, equally importantly, that you knew not to cram it all into the seminar. It is unlikely that you will be presenting a seminar on a completely arbitrary topic and so your research can also go into a future assignment.

Keep to time, without fail. If you have divided the seminar into presentation, activity, discussion then do not be tempted to cut into each section's time as this will feel rushed and unfulfilling. It is better that you adapt your presentation as you go, editing out less relevant information. This is information you can share in a handout after the seminar so it will not be lost. If you have three activities planned but feel that time is running out, then you could divide the group and give each small group a different activity which they can then feed back to the whole group, or you can simply cut out an activity entirely. This is something that is quite challenging to do on the spur of the moment so might be worth thinking about whilst you are planning. Remember to mention you did this in your reflective work, if you are asked to complete a reflection, and explain why you chose to cut the activity you did.

Try to have two or three clear questions that you are aiming to cover. You may wish to share these aims with the group at the start of your seminar. This will give the seminar a strong focus and ensure that each aspect gets plenty of time. A conclusion or summing up of the discussions is a useful way to end the seminar and may also lead you to posing a parting question for everyone to go away and consider.

Prepare some – but not too much – extra material ready for the Q&A/discussion part of the session. This is particularly important online as, in a classroom, students may feel awkward during a silence and feel more pressure to contribute, whereas online, with their camera turned off, they can feel 'hidden', reducing the sense of responsibility to talk. Face-to-face communication also leads to a more flowing conversation as people read and engage with body language and facial expression. Being prepared with extra material will reduce those potential silent moments. Try a range of open and closed question types to initiate discussion. Control as much as possible what you can prepare prior to the seminar so that you appear confident and capable.

If you are worried that there will be silence once you have finished your presentation, ask a friend to offer you a starting question. This can help break the ice and start a discussion. The chances are that everyone attending your seminar will also be leading a seminar that term and therefore you can persuade them to talk in your seminar if you talk in theirs. Be friendly and give them time to type in the comments or raise their hands. Ask a question, then say you are going to give them some time to think whilst you give a bit more information; this takes the immediate pressure off them to think of something and they are more likely to respond if given time to think.

We have noticed that students tend to worry about leaving pauses or silences in their seminars and so waffle through what could be a valuable opportunity for their peers to think and process what they have learned. Try silently counting to five once you have asked a question to see if leaving that space helps other students to find their voices.

Remember, when presenting, one of the most engaging aspects is if the presenter is clearly enthusiastic about the topic so it is good to show how you feel, to some extent. Summarise and respond to each point or several similar points raised. This shows that you are listening and responding to the discussion and allows you to showcase your knowledge on the topic as well as, hopefully, moving the discussion forward and bringing it to a conclusion.

What do students think?

Student quotes

'I felt the time went too quickly because we had too much material when we had to present it online. We forgot to factor in the time delay of screen sharing and setting up groups.'

'I really enjoyed being able to set everything up in a familiar place and I knew where to find everything.'

'I forgot to look at the chat and realised I had missed questions so had to rush and answer them at the end.'

'We realised that working in a pair was easier because, whilst one of us presented, the other could check the comments and feed it back into the discussion at the right moment.'

Moving ahead

Reflect on your experience and consider what you enjoyed and what you would do differently if you were to lead a seminar in the future. There may not be a reflective assignment linked to your seminar, but a small amount of reflection is useful in identifying the skills you have learnt for the future. It could help you during a job interview to be able to say that you can manage group discussions; it will be useful to have had this experience if you want to use an online sharing platform such as OneDrive in the future; it may be that you really enjoy leading seminars and creating activities, and this could feed into your thinking about your career plans. These are all skills you now possess and will be able to use in future projects.

4

Online assessed learning journals

The learning journal format of assessment is a great way to build up a collection of your work, to demonstrate your learning and to develop through ongoing feedback. If you are anxious when it comes to other forms of assessment, you may find learning journals a relaxing assessment process. An online learning journal can be constructed in one of three ways. Either it can be entirely hosted and written online, and you will be expected to log into it to complete pieces of work, or you will use it as a storage space where you can upload files. The last option is that you may have some pieces of work that you are expected to complete within the online learning journal system, and also to upload files that you have created outside of the journal.

ONLINE
BENEFIT

Assessed learning journals (before they moved online) were a collection of documents that could include text, diagrams, charts and pictures. Online learning journals can also include film clips, audio files, recorded presentations and animations.

Online assessed learning journals offer your lecturer a chance to monitor and guide you on your learning journey in a more hands-on way. If you have ever felt distanced from your lecturers and wished to be able to get more guidance, this would be the perfect opportunity for it. As the learning journal is added to, your lecturer will be able to assess and give feedback at regular intervals. It is a good idea to check at which points through the module or course your lecturer is planning to review your journal so that you can make sure it is all in order. This will be particularly important if you are someone who often completes their work just before the deadline.

LECTURER'S VIEW

An online learning journal is like an ongoing conversation between you and your lecturer, and it is a good opportunity for us to see the individual capabilities and needs of each student, so we are keen on this form of assessment.

The many and varied features that an online learning journal will offer you may seem alluring but, before you dash in and use them all, check what formats your lecturer would like to see. You may be very confident and comfortable with the platform, but your lecturer might still be getting to grips with it. Lecturers may have opted for particular formats because they suit the task best and following their guidance is the safest course of action. If there is something you would particularly like to put into your journal that has not been directed by your lecturer, simply ask if it would be okay so that they know what they are expecting to see from you.

ONLINE BENEFIT

Goal setting is usually a feature of online assessed learning journal platforms and is an excellent way of keeping on top of your output.

If, like us, you love the idea of goal setting, to-do lists and seeing the bigger picture in smaller chunks, then you will enjoy this feature of the journal. You may be given goals or be expected to establish them yourself, depending on your course requirements. The goals will be matched against the assessment criteria, so as you work through them you will know that you are on track to succeed. If you are responsible for your own goal setting, then be sure to make those goals SMART (specific, measurable, attainable, relevant and time-based). You will have a better chance of meeting your targets if they are SMART.

An example of a SMART goal is:

By week 8 of the Spring term, I will write a 500-word learning journal entry about what I have learnt from my academic placement.

In this example we have been *specific* about what it will be about, we have made it *measurable* because we have said it will be 500 words, it is *attainable* as we are confident that we can do this within the timeframe, it is *relevant* to our assessment as it is related to our academic placement and it is *time-based* because we have stated it needs to be completed by week 8 of the Spring term. We find that it is better to put the timeframe at the start of our goal writing because it is the thing that we, and others, most often forget to put in.

Think about making longer- and shorter-term goals so that you can pace your work nicely. If you prefer shorter-term projects, setting these objectives will suit your need to tick things off your to-do list. Conversely, if you enjoy longer-term projects, then the drawn-out nature of a learning journal will suit you. In these ways, a learning journal is a good assessment for most students.

ONLINE BENEFIT

Goal setting is something that can be shared with your lecturers so that it is easy for them to see where you will go next in your learning journey, as well as knowing which assessment criteria you are working towards achieving.

What is an assessed learning journal designed to show?

Skills

Five skill areas will be key to your success in online learning journals:

- Understanding the brief
- Setting SMART goals
- Gathering the relevant material
- Working in different, engaging formats
- Proof-reading

We will be covering all these areas in this chapter.

Knowledge

Having a clear understanding of how the online learning journal platform works (its functionality) and how your lecturer wants you to use it (how it will function as part of your assessment) is key to acing this online assessment. You should browse the learning journal platform and try out some of the features before you begin producing anything, if you can.

ONLINE
HURDLE

Sometimes it is not your technical skill that is the challenge here, it is just the thought of trying out something new with such an important project. That is why we would encourage you to carry out some initial platform browsing with a fellow student beside you, so that you both point out useful features and encourage each other.

A learning journal is designed to showcase your skills in terms of presentation of your work as well as to record and track your learning journey. This method of assessment offers you a fantastic opportunity to present your research and knowledge to your lecturers and these skills will be useful in your career too. You could liken it to when you are asked in mathematics to show your workings as well as your answer; in this case your lecturer wants to see your breadth and depth of knowledge and understanding.

Top tip

Keep on top of recognising, recording and reflecting on the transferable skills you are learning; this is important for your future employability.

What is involved?

When approaching an online learning journal, you may be asked to submit work in formats with which you are not very familiar. For example, you could be asked to submit a film clip or an audio file. It is crucial that you treat this piece of work in the same way you would treat an essay in terms of preparation. Following this checklist will help you to produce a good quality piece of work:

- Plan your work against the assessment criteria.
- Select appropriate formats for each entry to your journal (this may be directed by your lecturer).
- Produce the work to the best of your ability, giving yourself enough time at each stage.

- Check it against the assessment criteria again and proof-read it.
- Submit it in the required way by the deadline.
- Watch for feedback.

How is the online version different?

As with anything that is new to you, you should take some time to get used to it and to understand how you might use it going forward to best suit you.

You will want to make your learning journal as interesting as possible and so you might turn to additional pieces of software to produce material. Remember, if you do not pay for a service then you may find that what you produce is either limited or not as private as you want it to be; this may be fine for what you are doing but check the privacy notices of any software you are using. Be wary about paying for software or apps too early on in your learning journey as you could find they are not very useful or are incompatible with your university's Virtual Learning Environment (VLE) or learning journal platform. The platform on which you will be producing/recording your learning journey is likely to have everything you need, so not rushing to use other software is a sensible idea.

A true learning journal should reflect your trials, errors and achievements: showing only polished and final versions of your work defeats the object of a learning journal. The nature of it being online can sometimes tempt students into reworking their material based on feedback they receive from their lecturer, but unless you are asked to change it after feedback or to show multiple copies of a piece of work, try to leave it as an accurate record of your work at that moment in time.

LECTURER'S VIEW

Often online assessment platforms and VLEs have a tool that allows the lecturer to see for how long you have viewed your feedback or a resource. It can be disappointing when you do not read the feedback as it tends to show in later pieces of work. Feedback is a gift: it helps you to improve, so read it carefully and take the action points from it into your future work.

You might be expected to fill in a digital logbook, which is a way of recording your attendance at a workplace or similar. This is particularly useful in vocational courses and courses that have a work placement element to them as you might need to prove that you have done a certain number of hours there.

What challenges might this bring?

Something that you might find difficult with an online learning journal is the fact that it is not tangible. Online learning journals are not set up for printing out in the way a Word document or presentation can be. However, the benefit of an online system is that it is accessible from anywhere you have an internet connection, often including your phone. Be careful with this wonderful accessibility because it can be tempting to upload work before it is polished and ready to be seen.

Are there benefits to me with the online version?

An online learning journal has the benefit of being very mobile and easy to use. If you were away from your desk or campus and wanted to upload something, you could do it very easily. Most online assessment platforms have a plagiarism checker, which is beneficial to you as it will flag up any issues and you will have a chance to change them or reference correctly.

The various features afforded to you by an online learning journal mean that you may be able to set goals, see progress and reflect on your work more easily. Learning journals that are not online can often feel like bottomless pits of hard work, but an online learning journal allows you an overview of your body of work, so you can identify gaps and plug them.

LECTURER'S VIEW

Online learning journals offer you the chance to be efficient and focused with your work and they can be a real pleasure to make and to mark. An online learning journal gives us a clear understanding of what you can produce and so we find it easier to give you guidance should you need it.

What do I need to know?

Before you start

Be clear about how the learning journal platform works so that you can approach it with confidence. You need to be sure of the aims and objectives of the assessed learning journal and you will need to find out if the aims and objectives will change as the process goes on. For example, it may be that there is an overarching aim for your journal but that there are milestone aims as you go along. Alternatively, your journal may be broken into sections with different aims and objectives and, therefore, different assessment criteria. Read through the assessment criteria, if needs be several times over a few days, so that you know what is required of you to achieve good marks.

Check with your lecturer how much work should be added and when you need to do this. We sometimes find students either start or finish the academic year producing a large volume of work (either due to a fit of enthusiasm or sudden-onset anxiety), but struggle to maintain a steady flow of work. This certainly is not a huge problem if all the work is completed, but a learning journal is like a marathon and should be paced as such if you are going to gain maximum benefit in terms of developing your learning and skills. Knowing how often you are expected to upload work will give you a good idea of how to fit your journal output into your timetable along with your other work and commitments. It is a good idea for you to plan when you will be working on your journal so that you can relax, safe in the knowledge that it is achievable and will keep moving along.

Top tip

By finding out when and how you will receive feedback, you will know what dates you are working towards and you will be able to make space in your schedule to read and internalise the feedback you receive. This will be important to your ongoing work.

It is helpful if you can see an exemplar of what you should be producing so that you can be confident in your work. If there is not an example or a past learning journal available, you may need to request feedback on your early uploads to the journal to be sure that you are on the right track. Specific questions get specific answers so do not be shy about asking your lecturer, academic tutor or study support advisor questions such as 'At what level do you think I am working at this stage?', 'What do I need to do in this piece of work to improve my marks?', 'Does this meet criterion x?'

Top tip

If you are shown an example of a learning journal entry, check what grade it was given as it may be an average grade and you might be setting your sights higher.

As you go along

Keep referring to the aims, objectives and assessment criteria as you go along. Long, drawn-out assessment types can run the risk of becoming unfocused, so be careful not to lose sight of what is needed from you.

Top tip

Using key words from the assessment criteria/aims/objectives in your work will make it easier to see which assessment criteria you are meeting or trying to meet.

Allow yourself space and time to produce each learning journal entry and focus on just the entry you set out to complete, as this will keep you focused rather than overwhelmed. The risk of a long project such as a learning journal is that you will lose sight of the overall aim, resulting in an unfocused and disjointed piece of work. By keeping to carefully thought-out SMART goals, you are more likely to end up with a coherent journal with a clear learning journey recorded.

When you complete an entry, make a plan of what you intend to do the next time you will be sitting down to produce one. In this way you will keep up the momentum of your studies and be able to remain calm, knowing it will all be completed on time.

If you receive feedback that you do not understand or that you feel unsure about how to implement in subsequent pieces of work, find out whom you should approach for advice. This could be your lecturer, an academic tutor or a study support advisor. Communication is a two-way process and requires understanding on both sides, so be assertive if you are unsure about feedback you have received.

LECTURER'S VIEW

It is supremely helpful if you know what you want to get out of a meeting with your lecturer, or another member of staff, from the outset. By planning what you want to ask or say, you save time and you can be sure that, by the end of the meeting, you will have the knowledge you need to continue.

If you have a meeting with a lecturer or study supporter about your learning journal, take notes or ask someone into the meeting (such as a friend or notetaker) to do so. This summary of the meeting will be valuable to you going forward as it will remind you what you need to do next or whom to go to if you need further assistance.

Top tip

Keep copies of your work on a USB, a cloud or a device so that you have a back-up should you need it. This will also prove useful if you want to share anything with your future employers in an interview task such as a presentation.

Find out if you are allowed or expected to rework your material as you go along; if you are allowed to do this, you may find it a curse or a blessing as it will take more time and requires you to rework your material based on feedback, which can feel challenging. However, it also allows you to improve your marks and you will continue to develop the skill of utilising feedback effectively. The overall timeline will be important to you as you will need to keep on top of it so that you can produce your best work for the journal. There is a risk of feeling that an online learning journal is less formal, therefore less important than an exam. However, you might find it is harder to do well because your lecturer/assessor will know that you have had ample time and access to additional resources to complete it.

Top tip

A learning journal is an excellent record of your work to keep and share with potential employers as at least some of the entries might be relevant to your career. Check if you are allowed to do this as some universities have a policy about when your work can be shared.

Where do I go for help?

You may feel out of reach of your traditional forms of support if you are not on campus. However, you have a wealth of information at your fingertips. Online platforms generally have a help section and online communities to answer all sorts of questions. Your institution will have chosen the learning journal platform that they believe will suit its students and subjects best and there will be advisors and support staff prepared to help you. Check who these people are, and how you can get hold of them, and look for online help through your university as your first port of call. If you have a query related to the content of the learning journal, go to your lecturer. Otherwise go to the support staff in the first instance.

Top tip

> Do not wait too long before you seek assistance if you are struggling. Your enthusiasm for your learning journal may wane in the meantime and this will show in the quality of your work and your productivity, almost without you realising that this is happening to you.

You might be more knowledgeable on the technology being used for learning than some staff are, so consider asking a classmate or study buddy if the technology is getting in the way of your productivity. You might, for example, find that hyperlinks are inserted in different ways on differing platforms, or that the option to share with others is more complicated than you had expected on the platform you are using. Class groups tend to create WhatsApp groups or similar so that they can keep in touch and support each other with queries such as this.

ONLINE
HURDLE

It can be very easy to find yourself a member of multiple student WhatsApp groups, many of which will have been set up just for a single project. You might feel awkward if you message the wrong group, or you could find it stressful trying to juggle groups. Once a project is complete, consider exiting the WhatsApp group that was set up for it, unless you have found other reasons to stay.

Class groups online are an excellent way to get your queries answered swiftly outside of work hours, but be cautious: it is easy enough to check whether you are being given the correct technical advice to fix a glitch by trying it out; it is far more dangerous to assume that your fellow students can give you detailed advice on the assessment criteria, or hand-in dates. If you are at all unsure about the friendly advice you are being offered, double-check with a member of staff.

What should I do before I submit this at the final deadline?

You should check that you have completed all the required pieces of work; this is particularly important for this type of assessment as you will have collated several files for submission. You should allow time for proof-reading, but this is something that is easy to dismiss, particularly if you are running short of time. Proof-reading is an opportunity to improve your work, to correct any mistakes and to tie together your assignments to create a coherent body of work. Part of this review process should include a check for readability. Readability includes three elements: everything should be in the right order, you should ensure that there is nothing missing (from words missing in the title to whole documents or files that you require for your learning journal) and you need to be assessing whether the language you have used is easily readable. In Microsoft Word there is an editing function where the software checks the readability of your document. If you use this then just be careful to also make your own judgements on the suggestions it is making as it is not always perfectly right.

Top tip

Incorporating words and phrases from the assessment criteria will make your work easy to mark as you will have flagged up the key points in your material that match the criteria.

How do I get higher marks?

You are sure to be wondering how you can get higher marks in your assessed learning journal. We think that the following list will help you produce your best work:

- Follow the instructions and regularly refer to them.
- Manage your time carefully with SMART goals and self-imposed deadlines.
- Get feedback on your early additions to the learning journal.
- Alter your future submissions based on feedback.
- Proof-read your work.
- Go above and beyond the instructions if it is appropriate and feasible to do so.
- Utilise the features available to you on the platform.
- Respond to feedback as you go along.

What do students think?

'I loved creating my online learning journal. It was so satisfy-ing to see it all come together as I went along.'

If you are new to online learning journals you might find them a challenge to begin with. Some students love them and some dislike them; this is simply down to learning preferences. If you enjoy collating your work as you go along, if you tend to get your work well underway before deadlines and take joy in using multiple formats in your work, you are more likely to find online learning journals suit you and your way of working. If you prefer to do your work in the last few days before a deadline, then you could find the longevity of a learning journal assessment to be more problematic.

'It was a nightmare at the start because I had to learn how to use the system properly. I got there finally and loved playing around with it in the end.'

Learning journals work better through online platforms and the multiple fea-tures offered on them cater to a wider range of learning preferences. Students have told us that their online learning journal seemed more compli-cated at the start and that they needed time to get used to the system, and so you should plan in time to become acquainted with it in advance of your submission dates.

The benefit of having an online journal is that there is the opportunity to col-lect several pieces and types of work in one place, which can be accessed from anywhere there is an internet connection. Students have told us that they have found it satisfying to see their journal filling up and that it was easier to be able to see the assessment criteria on the system alongside their work. However, the drawback some students have identified is that it can be difficult to stop reworking bits and to make it a true reflection of the learning journey, rather than a polished finished article. A learning journal (online or otherwise) requires you to expose your weaknesses or errors to demonstrate your learning journey and reflective practice and this does not always feel comfortable to do.

Student quote

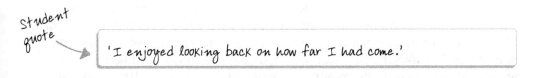

'I enjoyed looking back on how far I had come.'

As with all assessment types, you should find out how to utilise the format type to make it work for you. If you are completing something online but you need to proof-read a hard copy because you find it easier, then do so. If you find accessing question papers or assessment criteria a challenge online, then you should consider moving the text into a document that you can enlarge, alter the colour or print out.

Student quote

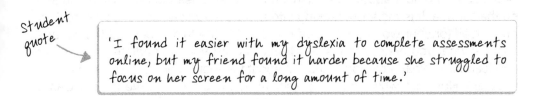

'I found it easier with my dyslexia to complete assessments online, but my friend found it harder because she struggled to focus on her screen for a long amount of time.'

You may find accessibility a hurdle and speaking to a member of staff in your university in the first instance will help you gain access quicker. Flagging up any additional learning need you have with the relevant department in your university will give you the best chance to get support in place for your studies and assessment, including online assessments. It might be a disability that does not limit you in on-campus assessments but does become an issue for online assessments, so talk with your university about it as soon as you can to get support set up.

Moving ahead

Learning journals comprise a steady collation of materials and this assessment format offers you the chance to hone multiple skills. In terms of your transferable skills, an online learning journal (if used to its fullest extent) can help you develop and become confident in producing and presenting your work in a variety ways. You may get the chance to film and upload a presentation or vlog, to write a short essay or blog, to complete a short-answer or multiple-answer test, to support your work with an audio commentary, and so much more. To maximise the benefits from completing an online learning journal, you should try to use as many of the formats as your lecturer/subject/platform allow and you should take a note of the skills you are learning for future reference when considering your employability.

Part of the process of a learning journal is reflection. The skill of reflection is something that should not be underestimated as it will prove important in your studies, your work and your life. All too often reflection as part of an assessment is dismissed or forgotten by students because they have not been shown the value of it. However, to be truly successful, you should complete each part of your learning journey with a spot of reflection to be able to move onto the next stage effectively.

You might need to complete a reflection activity as part of your learning journal. If you are issued an activity, it is sensible to assess whether it has helped you at all. If not, you may want to reflect in a different way, which is fine but worth checking with your lecturer.

Reflection is not just about looking in a mirror and repeating back what you see on the surface. It is more like looking into a pond – you can see a representation of yourself (or your work) on the surface, but it is the things beyond the surface that are what you need to consider. Think beyond your immediate assessment and feedback: What have you found out about the topic/your learning preferences/yourself? How can what you have discovered benefit you in the future? Can a weakness be reduced? Have you found skills that you did not realise you had? Did you enjoy that assessment format? What were the consequences of your learning journey to that point? These are just some of the questions that will help you to think more deeply about your learning journey and will offer you a more robust and worthy reflection on your work.

Almost every reflection point should have an action attached to it, to make it worthwhile, as illustrated in Table 4.1.

Table 4.1   How to produce an action point from reflection

Reflection	Action
I found it difficult to write a learning journal entry every week as I would forget what I had learnt at the start of the week by the time I came to write it on a Friday.	Keep a notebook so that I can jot down learning points through the week or use an app such as OneNote or Sticky Notes to help me to keep track of them.
I enjoyed producing a short film clip to put in my learning journal, but it took several attempts to get it perfect.	I will plan what I am going to say before I turn the camera on.
I keep missing the deadlines I set myself.	I will add an extra week onto each deadline I have set if I can.

Reflection is a key skill that is useful beyond your studies. In terms of employ-ability, this is an important asset. Being able to recognise what is going well and what needs to be changed relies on effective reflection. Assessed online learning

journals provide an excellent opportunity for you to gain skills beyond the immediate assessment, as they give you the chance to produce materials that you
could use in an interview or work setting. They give you the chance to hone
academic and transferable skills, and you can build your academic capabilities
steadily throughout, potentially with more feedback than you are likely to get
through other assessment methods. Recognising all of this, and understanding
how to best utilise a learning journal, will help you to enjoy the process, confident
that you are achieving what you set out to do when you first came to university:
to improve academically and prepare yourself for a successful career.

5

Online assessed portfolios

An assessed portfolio is a body of work collected by a student over a long period of time that showcases their knowledge and skills, matching the marking criteria set out at the start of the project. It can be created in a number of ways and include various aspects. However you decide to present your portfolio, at its core, it should include samples of your work, self-analysis and comment on this work, and future goal setting.

An assessed portfolio can include any or all of the following:

- Aim or hypothesis (mandatory) – consider what the portfolio is trying to showcase.
- Samples of the student's work.
- Learning journal or diary entries to reflect on the learning journey.
- Research material – this should be an analysis of what is already out there.
- Essays – these might be assessed separately and then included in the portfolio.
- Images, videos or audio.
- Presentations – these might be assessed separately and then included in the portfolio.
- Notes on tutor–student discussions – these might lead you down a new path of exploration on the topic.
- Conclusion (mandatory).

What is an assessed portfolio designed to show?

Skills

A portfolio is a long-term project that has a unique ability to showcase not only knowledge but also the presentation of materials, development of ideas, and your ability to research and choose appropriate material. A portfolio may include other forms of assessments such as presentations, short-answer tests and vivas or professional discussions. Collecting, creating and presenting this material can be a challenge but it is worthwhile as a portfolio can be used not only for a single module or course but also as a representation of your work for future employers. We were pleased to find recently that this was the case for a student who had graduated four years ago. She told us: 'I have used my portfolio in interviews more than any other example of my work, because so much is crammed in there that can show off my work.'

For an online portfolio you will need to show your skills in identifying the aims of the portfolio and how you might achieve these, recognising relevant material and collating this in a meaningful way, and being able to present this in a multi-media format online. Your portfolio should start with a clearly stated aim followed by a breakdown of the methods you will use and your expected findings. Then you can start your research and present your findings. A portfolio can then finish with a conclusion and a statement about how you will be moving forward with the knowledge you have gained.

A portfolio might not be simply a written document; it could be a collation of your work such as a photography portfolio or a theatre portfolio, which will demonstrate your developing skills, not only to your assessor but also to a future employer.

LECTURER'S
VIEW

Portfolios are a large body of work and can therefore be a daunting prospect. We often suggest to our students that they create a timetable of when they will be working on it and what they will have achieved at each marker in their timetable. It is nigh on impossible to create a portfolio of work all at once and so the key is building it little by little.

Knowledge

A good knowledge of the topic is vital, but this is something that is likely to develop through your portfolio building so is not necessary at the outset. It is important however to have a very clear understanding of what the portfolio is aiming to capture and therefore you should have a strong idea of how to start your research. This information should be given to you in your assignment brief but if you need clarification, it is best to ask your lecturer early on. You can also check in with your peers to see how they are approaching the task but be aware there might be several ways of interpreting the brief; a portfolio is very much an individual expression of your ideas.

Knowledge of online portfolio resources and platforms is useful to have prior to putting your information together. Your institution will have a Virtual Learning Environment (VLE) that you could use for this, but it might not be sophisticated or creative enough for what you are planning to produce. It is worth having a look around online for different presentation platforms such as OneNote or Xerte but you could also make a website to showcase your work using Wix or create a YouTube channel if you are creating screencasts. Consider the material you want to share and then judge which platform suits your needs. If you are unsure, ask around to see what others are using and always make sure that your lecturers or tutors are happy with your choice.

You may also want to find an appropriate method of storing your research such as OneNote, Google Drive or Dropbox. Be aware that some of these services will charge you or have data limits so it is worth looking around for the best service for you. Consider whether you will use this method for other aspects of your online life. You can also use file transfer services such as WeTransfer and TransferNow if you want to share files or folders with someone.

Top tip

Finding a suitable online storage space for your research can be useful, not only for your coursework, but also for your future employment and other areas of your digital life.

If you want your lecturer or peers to access your work throughout the development of your portfolio then you will need to consider how you want to share this information. On Google Drive, for example, you can create a shared folder that allows you to give permission to anyone you invite to see, comment or edit any of your work that is in the folder. Equally you can share file by file meaning that you can give different permission to different people. Test these different options out with a friend first if you are unsure how these permissions might work and how your work may look on another computer.

ONLINE HURDLE

Take the time to explore the different platforms out there and watch tutorials on how they work and how to utilise all their functions before deciding which platform, or platforms, would most suit your learning style and work.

Engagement

Engagement with the material you are researching will become obvious through your work, but you should consider how you want to show your engagement. For example, putting all your research material into a folder does not prove you have digested any of the information or allowed it to affect your own opinions. A better way to show engagement would be to put forward your own hypothesis, carry out the research to either back up or negate your hypothesis, and then comment on this research and how it has moved you forward in your understanding of the topic.

As part of your portfolio building, you will undoubtedly engage with external resources as you research your topic and you can be creative with how you present this: a typed diary of your experiences can be interesting, but a photo can be a nice visual addition. Equally you may choose to film yourself presenting your ideas or create a video montage of research. An example of this could be to create a video montage of the same scene from *Romeo and Juliet* but performed in numerous ways to show how interpretation of a script can be dependent on societal and theatrical norms of the day as well as the directors' overall vision for the play.

This type of visual insertion is, of course, much easier to include in an electronic document or on a platform than it would be if you were relying on a hard copy submission.

Adding visual elements is beneficial to a portfolio to make it stimulating but you also want to make these stimuli relevant to your work, not just an add on, as this will help to boost your marks. Online portfolios offer an array of presentation methods such as video clips, pictures, audio recordings and typed work. You can use links, quizzes and templates to create a really beautiful, eye-catching and engaging piece of work.

In our opinion, it is much more engaging to see a portfolio which uses a variety of ways to present the work, creating an interesting and informative portfolio. It is important to be consistent in some aspects to create a coherent narrative throughout the work. We have seen students who present their work with clear introductions and conclusions to each sub-topic within their portfolio, which makes for a clear narrative to follow. Other students have inserted video clips, pictures and audio files alongside their written research. This extra dimension can succinctly demonstrate their point and is a nice addition to their work.

___

You may also engage with external supporters and resources and online is a great way to link to them quickly. You can include a link to someone else's website for further information or to a video clip proving a point in your research. You could also contact professionals or peers as part of your research, but be warned that, although sending an email can be quick, getting a response in a timely manner, or at all, is not guaranteed. You will also need to complete an ethics and consent form before including other people in your research. It is important to curate your resources and ensure they are relevant to your portfolio, so keep going back to the original criteria and checking that all your information is relevant.

When working on a portfolio it can be tempting to use all your information as you do not want to waste anything but the benefit of working online is you can store all this information and make it easily accessible to you at a later date. If you are sharing something like a Google Drive or Microsoft OneDrive folder with your assessor, then you could put a folder in there with additional research meaning they can see your process and what you have been working on that might not have ended up in the final portfolio. Part of creating a portfolio is knowing what not to put in your final piece.

Table 5.1 shows an example of how activities could be spaced out across the development of a portfolio, to give you a sense of the rhythm of the work as it develops.

Table 5.1   Example of an activity table for portfolio building

Activity	Deadline	Completed	Notes
Write aims	Week 1	/	
Create ethical consent forms and confirm with tutor	Week 2	/	Make sure it covers all the questions I want to ask... maybe make a list first before writing the consent form... Check with tutor
Identify whom I want to interview	Week 2	/	
Send out consent forms	Week 3		
Arrange and hold interviews	Week 4		Online or face-to-face?
Record and analyse results	Week 5		Quantitative or qualitative data?
Plan next section	Week 5		

Sharing

Sharing information is an important part of creating any portfolio as you need to know that you are going down the right path otherwise you can waste too much time. Sharing information with your lecturer throughout the process is usual and you will often have short-term deadlines imposed throughout the process so be aware of when these are and what your lecturer will be expecting to see at these points. You can also use these deadlines as an opportunity to meet with your lecturer, show your work and propose your next stage of work as these regular check-ins will help to guide you to a successful portfolio that matches the marking criteria.

You may also wish to share your portfolio, or parts of it, with peers and even strangers. Be prepared for feedback and productive criticism when you are sharing your work. Online can be a great way of sharing your work far and wide but it also means it will be under scrutiny from other people working in your area, so you need to examine each part of it for accuracy and ensure you have a robust referencing system so that you do not accidently plagiarise or misquote someone.

If you would like to invite discussion or comments on your work, it is worth considering how you might go about doing this: will this be something you put up on YouTube or are you going to put a poll out on Facebook?

Top tip

Think carefully before engaging with external people and work out exactly what you want to gain from the interaction.

What is involved?

Once you have established the parameters of your portfolio you will start to collate information from several sources; this might be from secondary sources such as books, journals and online articles and it might also be first-hand research such as going to see a performance or attending a conference or online seminar on your chosen topic. Whatever the original sources of the material, the thing they all have in common is they will need to be recorded and stored somewhere for later referencing.

At the start of any project you invariably have a wide research field until you can narrow it down and incorporate it into your work. There are several ways of storing information, but the most important thing is to organise your research in such a way that you can easily find what you are looking for when you go back to look for it. This may be saving documents on a hard drive and making sure you write the topic and the date you found it as the file name. It may be that you want to save it to the Cloud so that you can find it on any computer at any point. In addition to producing single documents, you might want to create folders and subfolders to help keep your thinking clear and your material organised.

If you have real-life objects such as a book you want to save a few pages from, then it is worth scanning and saving it as a digital copy so all your material is in the same place. The same applies to play brochures or posters that you may want to reference. You might find that your library already has an electronic copy of these and therefore it is worth contacting your library for assistance. You can either scan them in or take a photo and email it to yourself before uploading it to the Cloud. In this way you will always be able to access the document copy of whatever it is you have photographed and then you can place it into your portfolio.

Top tip

Make sure you are clear as to why your research is relevant, particularly if you are collecting material and artefacts to include in your portfolio. A brief explanation of why you have included the item will help to justify its place in your portfolio.

A portfolio is much like a scrap book in the sense you can stick in all the items that you found relevant on your journey as long as you comment on why they are relevant.

There are a number of ways to present your work and, as we mentioned before, it is worth exploring your options and considering what it is you might want to show before plumping for a specific platform. It might be that you want to set up on a couple of platforms such as creating a Vimeo channel to show off your Prezis and also setting up a Google Drive account to save all your documents in a neatly labelled folder so your lecturer can look through your work. When laying out your work you should make sure to label each file clearly. You might choose to set up folders in date order or based on subject matter but, whichever way you choose to go, make sure it is clear to the assessor in what order they should view your work. You might want to ask a friend to check this before you submit your work as, although it might be clear in your mind, it might be difficult for someone coming to it fresh.

If you want to present your work in the form of a slide show, such as Microsoft PowerPoint, then you have the benefit of being able to make voice recordings for your slides as well as using automatic captions creating an accessible presentation. Other services do offer this, so it is worth looking around for what would suit your work the best. When you prepare your slides remember you can add video clips, links and voice recording to make it a well-rounded and impressive presentation. Using the voice recording means you do not, and indeed should not, put all your information on the slides. The slides are there as a way of highlighting the main points on which you will be elaborating in your spoken presentation.

Portfolio building can be a time-consuming and lengthy process and so it is best to be proactive and realistic at the start. Set aside time each week to research and to work on your portfolio; a little bit of time each week is much more manageable than working on it for a full week before the deadline. It is also much more fruitful to work on it bit by bit. A portfolio is designed to gather information about your processes as a researcher and presenter of information; it captures your thinking process and your discoveries much like a polished version of a learning journal. This can be a joyful exploration but only if you dedicate enough time to it and do not try to overload yourself either right at the start or at the end of the process. One of our graduates last year revealed: 'I spent more time on my portfolio than any other piece of work at uni, despite it being a second year project. I was glad that I gave myself enough time – I got completely engrossed!'

Create a timetable of your planned work and stick to it. The items on the timetable might change as your research takes you off on a tangent but try to stick to the timeframe as this will really help prevent you from spending too long procrastinating or putting off the work, which inevitably leaves you feeling stressed and dissatisfied. Taking your time each week also allows you to contact people and get their responses if you are undertaking first-hand research or if you require assistance with your project.

You will find that, if you make and stick to a timetable of work, and you store all your work in an orderly way, you will enjoy the meandering path of creating a unique portfolio. You can also use your creativity to produce a beautiful portfolio to match your style. A portfolio is as much about your journey in creating it as it is about gaining marks.

Top tip

Make sure that you tick off any paths of research you have finished exploring so you do not leave loose ends. This may be by writing a short statement in your portfolio, if you have included the research here, to say that you will not be taking this part of your research any further and explain why you have made this decision.

How is the online version different?

The main difference in creating an online portfolio as opposed to a hard copy portfolio is that you have more flexibility in how you create and present it. With a hard copy portfolio you generally have text and pictures as well as possibly a USB on which there might be videos or audio recordings. Online you can have all your multi-media work in a single place and can reach out to other websites, clips and research with a click of the mouse. It can be slicker to navigate and easier to share than with a hard copy. Multiple people can view it at the same time and be looking at different pages simultaneously. It is also easy to amend any mistakes or add information as you would not have to reprint a copy or add pages to your bound portfolio.

Working online will certainly feel different, but it can feel more achievable as you can upload material, link out to other sites or clips and quite quickly create a professional looking portfolio which might be useful for gaining work in the future. A paper version can cause chaos as you try to print all your material, upload videos on to a USB pen and bind it in a professional way. Once you have completed your online portfolio it might be that you go back to it a year later, update or change aspects of it and then use it for a professional project. You can also store all your research that you did not need on the Cloud ready to use in a later project, so nothing is wasted.

An online version may be accessed by your lecturer throughout its creation and therefore you may have working documents in which you can both track changes, or audio files with comments on, so you can work more collaboratively with your lecturer.

LECTURER'S VIEW

Students have shared information too early in the past and then struggled to organise their work and explain what it was that they actually wanted to share with us. They felt that the process of sharing too early was intrusive as they were not ready to share material, so make sure you consider when and how you want to share your work.

What do I need to know?

Do find out how you are expected to showcase your work and give clear instructions on how to access your work if you are using a platform your lecturer or assessor is not used to accessing. Your work may be a thing of beauty but if it is difficult to access or navigate then you will lose the goodwill of the assessor and also potentially lose marks for lack of clarity. Consider this as being a useful collation of your ideas and materials ready for a potential employer and therefore make it coherent, accessible and stylish. You could ask a friend to access your completed portfolio, or a part of it, to check its accessibility and clarity.

> **ONLINE HURDLE**

As there are a multitude of platforms online you can find that you end up in a muddle by not making coherent links, both hyperlinks and informational links, between your online pages. Always get someone to look through your work regularly to ensure you are presenting it in an accessible and coherent manner.

You will be given a deadline to collate your material and present it in a portfolio online, so it is worth checking the timescale and deadlines with your lecturer or in your handbook. A portfolio is usually created over a module, term or year and therefore there are likely to be deadlines for each stage of it throughout the time you have been given. Stick to these timings as they are there for a reason and can often be a good check-in point to ensure you are on the right track.

What challenges might this bring?

The most obvious challenge is learning how to use the software in the first place before you even start creating your portfolio. Picking the right software for what you want to achieve with your portfolio can be difficult, so do your research and see what is available. It might be that your lecturers have specified where they want your portfolio to be and therefore you can focus on learning how to use all the functions on that platform but, if they do not specify, then you need to do the research yourself. Ask your fellow students what they are planning to use or have used in the past and do watch tutorials on how to use different software: we promise it is worth it. Once you have identified a couple of platforms you might want to use, have a play around with them to see which feels most intuitive to you and then you can start putting your work onto them.

Top tip

> You might feel you are wasting time learning how to share your material online but it can also be fun and there are plenty of tutorials out there so take the time to watch them rather than stumbling through how to use the various functions in each platform. Do the research!

You need to keep in touch with your lecturers and send snippets of your work to ensure you are on the right path and also that you are presenting your work in a way they can access.

It is always worth considering what material you are collating and how this may best be presented before you start working on it. If you are collecting written articles you might want to label them in their own folder to make them easily accessible without having to open each one to know what is in it. If you have several video clips, the same applies. Review your methods of recording information occasionally, so that you can check that it is still pertinent information and still being presented and stored in the best possible way.

Group portfolios online can be a great collaboration of ideas but can also get visually messy, so be really clear about who is creating what material and how you are going to share it. At the end of the project make sure one or all of you work through the material creating a unified style and making sure there are no repetitions. Working and sharing material online can be an instant way to collaborate and can help to support group work; for example, if you find something pertinent to another group member's topic you can instantly send them the link. Equally, if you are sharing all your information all the time then it becomes very apparent if there are repetitions or if you are working at cross purposes. It is worth agreeing how you are going to share your work in your final product so that you can start shaping the work in a similar fashion to each other rather than trying to reshape it at the end of the project. Table 5.2 presents an example of how to organise building a group portfolio.

Table 5.2 Example of a shared activity and checklist table for group portfolio building

Activity	Who is responsible?	Deadline	Checked by the group and incorporated into the portfolio
Research literary influences on Shakespeare	Arrietty	January 15th	/
Historical context	Delphinium	January 15th	/
Stage performances through the years	Jacob	January 15th	/
Film performances through the years	Alouette	January 15th	/

Are there benefits to me with the online version?

There are several benefits to creating an online portfolio, including ease of access for both you and your lecturer or other group members if you are working in a group. This can save time as opposed to printing out information and physically taking it to your lecturer for review. You might find that you are able to fit creating an online portfolio into your life more easily than creating a hard copy portfolio as you can quickly add something whilst you are on your computer checking your emails or at the end of a lecture or seminar.

Recording all your research, notes and material on an online Cloud in one place also means you can access it from any computer wherever you find yourself, making it far easier to collate and update your research regularly. You may also find that any research that is not relevant for this portfolio can be saved and used for another project or assignment at a later date.

You can be creative with multi-media information to best suit your learning style, so, if you are a visual learner for example, you may find that you want to use videos and pictures to support your research and to show your research journey. You may prefer to talk about your work and so could create a video diary. If you have a mathematical brain you might like to use charts and diagrams to analyse your findings. There is something out there for everyone, so find the right software for your learning style and show off your work in a unique and interesting way.

When thinking about creating an online portfolio, remember that there are plenty of offline resources to use, such as libraries, live lectures and seminars, professional discussions and exhibitions. First-hand research can be time consuming, but it can be a very rewarding experience, especially if you have a clear aim. When accessing online information make sure you are visiting reputable sites and authenticated research and then reference these accurately and fully using the referencing system dictated by your course handbook.

Top tip

Learn to reference correctly at the start of your project otherwise you will have a laborious job trying to re-reference at the end of your project.

Where do I go for help?

As always, it is worth contacting your lecturers in the first instance should you require clarity on the portfolio topic and aims. Contact your IT support staff for assistance with IT-related issues. Your lecturers will be able to signpost you to relevant support staff should they not be able to assist you. Most online platforms have a 'frequently asked questions' section and video tutorials on how to use their software. You will also be able to find online communities to assist with technical queries.

Your peers will also be a great support system for you, not only in practical assistance on how to use online platforms, but also as a sounding board for your ideas and as study buddies to keep you on track with your proposed time-line. A study buddy can support you and you can support them; this can motivate you as when you are trying to keep them on track you ultimately keep yourself on track.

How should I prepare?

Prepare as you usually would in the sense of organising your timetable but make sure to give yourself extra time to explore different software and platforms. You may also need to allocate extra time to uploading your material into your port-folio if you are new to this software, although you are bound to get quicker as you become more practised.

Check the assessment criteria and how the lecturer is expecting to view your work as this may influence your design decisions and which platform you might use. Also check whether you are expected to include a diary, log or learning journal as part of your portfolio. A portfolio should be a collection of material that proves your learning against a list of criteria so make sure you know what these criteria are.

LECTURER'S VIEW

You may want to print out your material so you have a hardcopy as well as an online copy. Some students work better with physical material as opposed to all online and this is fine but be prepared that you may be giving yourself twice the work by creating a hardcopy and then having to upload or type it up.

Look at the suggested reading and resources list in your course handbook; there is a reason it is recommended, and it is a good starting point for your research. If you are accessing online resources, you can bookmark pages so you can revisit them at a later date. Bear in mind that some websites update their material or vanish entirely, so it is worth taking screenshots and including the date you visited the site in your references.

What should I do on the day of submission?

In your last-minute checks make sure that you can access everything and that you have 'shared' it. Have someone check that all your work is accessible as this can be different for the 'author' and for the 'viewer'. Once you have submitted your work it is worth noting down what you learned about creating a portfolio online and where you need to spend more time for future portfolios. It may be that you lost track of your proposed timetable or that you would have preferred more first-hand research opportunities; knowing these things will help you prepare for future assignments. Do get peer and assessor feedback on your portfolio as it is always useful to receive a range of responses.

How do I get higher marks?

Follow the instructions exactly. This is always a good idea, but especially important in this context as you do not want to lose marks by misinterpreting the assignment. Always try to stick to the timetable, whether this has been created by your lecturer or you, so you have plenty of time to complete the portfolio to the best of your ability. Also take the time to understand the software you are using as this ultimately saves you time later on.

Make sure you create a clear and thorough plan to follow. You may find that you deviate from this and that is okay – you can readjust your plan to suit your developing portfolio but starting with no plan will lead to a messy and incomplete portfolio, losing you marks.

Store any additional material you gather and reference really well so you can always go back should you need to use extra material at a later date. By doing this you will not waste any time searching for that great quote you found three months ago, and you will also be able to use your 'spare' research at some point. Research all adds to your understanding of the world and others' perspectives so is never a waste, but make sure you do not spend too much time researching something that is not relevant to your current assessment.

Top tip

Know when something is not relevant and put the book down, however interesting it may be. In the same way do not be afraid to trim your work to better suit your portfolio. A concise and meaningful portfolio is preferable to a messy and overly stuffed one.

What do students think?

Student quote

> 'By the time I handed in my portfolio, it really felt like mine. It was something that I had created from scratch, it looked exactly how I wanted it to be, and I am completely proud of what I have achieved.'

Students get emotionally attached to their portfolios, investing so much time and effort that they become a hugely important part of their university life and sense of achievement. Online portfolios seem to create even greater pride, because they can be made to look so professional when they are complete and are easily shared with family and friends.

Your portfolio is exactly that: yours, so create it in a style that suits you within the parameters of the assignment criteria. Think about how you would like to view your research and resources and create those for your portfolio. If you are a visual learner or prefer demonstrations then create videos, if you are a bookworm then create an essay, if you find sound really aids in your learning then create a voice recording over slides or make a film. Portfolios can be created in many different ways and there are numerous platforms out there on which to create your portfolio, so create something informative and unique to show off your learning.

Moving ahead

Take the time to reflect on your experience, considering what you enjoyed and found useful and what aspects you found challenging. Is there anything you would use again? Maybe you particularly enjoyed creating screencasts or Prezis and might use these in the future, or perhaps you relished first-hand research and being able to put these results into graphs and diagrams?

You should now have a range of online skills and be able to navigate online platforms. You are also able to organise, assess and store your research effectively. You can offer your work using a variety of multi-media presentation forms, and all of these should be recorded as transferable skills on your CV. Well done... you are now more employable, with a range of technical and practical skills under your belt.

6

Online assessed multiple-choice tests

Multiple-choice tests are a useful way to test your understanding on a fundamental level. They can be used to recall information, problem-solve and to differentiate between fact and opinion. They will not test your breadth and depth of knowledge like an essay-style question will, but they will give an assessor a clear idea of whether you have a fundamental understanding of the topic. Multiple-choice tests often coincide with short-answer assessments as this allows for the initial understanding to be tested and then elaborated upon.

In this chapter we will explore how an online test may vary from a live test and how you can prepare for these types of assessments.

LECTURER'S
VIEW

Multiple-choice tests are a useful barometer of knowledge learned and retained. We tend to use them as a formative assessment or alongside other assessment methods to test the full range of skills and knowledge a student has learned.

What is an online multiple-choice test designed to show?

Skills

The skill in answering a multiple-choice question is inevitably being able to decipher between the false, true and believable options given to you as answers. You will also need to make sure you read each question and instructions carefully as each question may ask you to tick one or more boxes and this can fluctuate throughout the exam.

A multiple-choice test requires you to be a confident decision-maker as you will have to have faith in your knowledge not to be left doubting yourself over some of the more plausible answer options.

Knowledge

The more knowledge you have the easier it will be to answer this test, but make sure you are revising the right area and do not make it too broad, otherwise you will not have the time or the headspace to take in all the information being tested in the assessment.

You will also need knowledge on what technology you will need to access the test and all its elements. This might mean taking time to explore the software, watching an online tutorial or having a meeting with your lecturer.

What is involved?

A standard online multiple-choice assessment can be a very effective and simple way to test your knowledge at that moment. You will be expected to revise the topic and then answer multiple-choice questions on it. Alternatively, you might be asked to take a stimulus-led assessment where you will be asked to watch a clip or read information and then answer the questions; this can sometimes be easier as you can do very little revising up to this point.

How is the online version different?

In a live setting you would be invited into the exam room under exam conditions and asked to complete the paper on the desk. In an online version you will be sent a link and given a limited time to access the test; for example, you may be asked to submit your answers within two hours of receiving this link. This can cause some confusion as this deadline is not necessarily how long you get given to complete the assessment but rather you have to access the link within that two-hour slot. Ensure you know the time allocated to complete the test once you have accessed that link. The online assessment may have restrictions such as not being able to pause once you have pressed play, as can be found with a driving theory or language receptive test, or you may only be able to tick one box and once the page has moved forward you cannot go back to change your answer. Some tests allocate your marks and allow you to re-sit immediately; this often happens with tests for online safeguarding courses as the aim of the test is to encourage you to discover information and then be able to retain the information.

You may get the option to go back and forth between the questions and therefore you can go through answering all those you find easier first before tackling the trickier questions, or vice versa. This is one of the strategies upon which you will need to decide. For some students, tackling the questions they find most challenging is best left to the end, when they have built their confidence, whereas others prefer to face the harder questions when they feel fresh and full of energy.

When completing an online multiple-choice test, it is worth asking your lecturer for a mock exam so you can see what the layout will look like and develop your strategy. Knowing what you are expecting to see on the screen can instil confidence and means you do not waste time working out how the test will function. Once you have received the mock you will know whether you are expected to complete an online form that has a different page for each question, whether there is a single document you are meant to download, fill in and then upload onto a system, and whether you can go back and forth between questions. Even simple things like knowing whether there is a timer in the corner of the screen or not can be beneficial.

Top tip

As some courses might have only recently moved online it may be that there are no mock assessments to view before your real assessment. In this case ask the lecturer to explain what you will see and how the exam is intended to proceed. This will give you some idea as to what to expect in your online assessment.

Some assessments will ask you to watch a short clip followed by a series of questions. In this case it would be useful for you to have a pen and paper nearby to jot down important information you have seen in the clip; this will help when you are asked the questions as you can look back at your notes as a reminder of what you saw. In this case there is no difference between a live and an online assessment. The difference will come when you have to input your answers on the computer; this may automatically appear on your screen during or at the end of the test, or you may need to download and then upload your answer sheet.

ONLINE
BENEFIT

As you are already using your computer to take the test, you could use a document or the 'sticky note' function on your computer to make notes as you go. That way, everything you do is on screen, which might make you feel more comfortable.

Once you have completed the test you will need to know how to submit your answers. It may be simply clicking on a 'submit' button, but it may mean uploading your answer sheet to a Virtual Learning Environment (VLE) or even emailing your lecturer your answers. Once you have submitted your test it is worth informing your lecturer or the administrative staff you have done this in case something goes wrong with the technology and they do not receive it (unless your learning system gives you a receipt for your submission).

You might find that an online multiple-choice test involves different types of questions such as drag-and-drop questions (you select and move the answer you believe to be correct), either/or type questions (sometimes known as closed questions) or fill-in-the-blank questions. Knowing what question types you might face is useful as it will help you prepare for your specific assessment.

What challenges might this bring?

An online multiple choice test requires you to be aware of how to access the exam rather than just turning up to the classroom at the required time. Make sure you know how the link to the exam works and whether there is a time deadline or whether the clip only plays once, for example. If this is the case, then be careful not to click the link until you are absolutely ready for your exam.

Practise exams online so you know what format you are expecting to see. It is tempting to rush through a multiple-choice exam as it is simply a case of ticking boxes, but they can be harder than they seem. Usually there is a choice of an obviously false answer, the right answer and a couple of plausible answers to test your exact knowledge of the topic. It can be difficult to detect the real answer when faced with plausible answers as well, so it is worth revising well for your exam and taking your time to complete and check your answers before submitting. As with any exam, preparation is the key to success. Make sure you know what the test will be assessing and then revise the topic thoroughly.

LECTURER'S
VIEW

Some students do not necessarily understand that multiple-choice assessments can be a real challenge when you are not fully confident with the material. Often the answers can be very nuanced and similar and so, unless you have revised, you could easily pick the wrong answer.

Another challenge to consider is the hardware you will be using to complete your exam. There are many ways of accessing online content with desktop computers, laptops, tablets, phones and so forth, but not all of them will access the content in the same way and, indeed, some of these devices might not be able to access your exam content at all. Check with your lecturer or IT support that your device will be able to access all the exam content and that, crucially, you will be able to interact with it.

Even if your phone will allow you to access and complete the assessment you may find that there are video clips being shown that will be very small on your phone screen compared to a laptop screen.

You may find that your WiFi is slow on your laptop but that your phone has a great connection and therefore you will be able to interact better with the exam content on your phone. Think about what will be best for you and if you have any queries go to your lecturer or IT department to clarify as soon as possible. Timeliness is key to resolving any potential access issues prior to the exam.

When considering access to online content you may have additional needs that require adjustments to be made; this may be in the form of larger writing, an interpreter or captions or extra time. You will need to ensure that you make your lecturer aware of these adjustments with plenty of time to put these in place. If you require additional support with a reader or interpreter, then they may wish to access the exam content prior to the exam date so they can prepare, or you could screen share via Zoom or Microsoft Teams so they can see your exam as you go through it and read or interpret as you work through the material.

Are there benefits to me with the online version?

One online benefit to multiple-choice exams is that you can set up your own working space and therefore the anxiety created by the exam room environment is reduced.

There are further benefits to completing a multiple-choice test online, the first of which is that you can start the test in your own time, and you do not have to worry about finding the right place before the exam starts. Although there may be some leeway on when you sit the test, do not allow yourself to become complacent. It is still important to establish exam conditions wherever you are so that you are not distracted from the test and can focus completely. You may feel more confident working in your own space and without the comparison of seeing other students finishing their exam before you.

The benefits continue. You will save time travelling to and from the exam as well as potentially having more flexibility on start and finish times for the exam. Quite often online multiple-choice exams will automatically grade themselves so you receive your mark quicker than paper tests, which will have to be manually marked by an assessor. Online tests are naturally more secure as they remove human error to a certain extent; the fewer people involved, the less risk there will be of losing the paperwork or making mistakes in the marking.

Should you need to re-sit the test you may get more flexibility in when you can sit this as you will not need your exams office or department to set up a room for you and to provide you with fresh answer papers. This means that re-sits can be easily accessed and quickly marked so there is less time between your revision and your re-sit, with less time to forget information.

What do I need to know?

As with any exam, you need to know what is being assessed through the test: is it factual information, assessing your interpretation of information or a mixture of both? In the case of multiple-choice questions quite often they are designed to test your knowledge on the subject either as an overall topic or in response to stimuli such as a video clip or presentation. These sorts of tests can assess long-term retention of information and attention to detail. In the case of a driving theory test, for example, the candidate is asked to know the Highway Code but will also be asked to identify hazards in a video clip. The same occurs in a language test: did you understand the overall context that Sav was giving you about going on a picnic, and did you identify the specific colour of the rug as green or red?

Knowing whether you are being tested in response to a stimulus you will be shown just prior to the test or whether you are being tested on previous learning is vital in knowing how best to prepare. If it is the case that you are being tested on previous knowledge, then revision of the topic is going to be paramount. If you are being asked to respond to a stimulus, then you can prepare through mock exams to give you a general idea as to what questions might be asked of you.

Where do I go for help?

With a classroom-based test you know that if something goes wrong then you will have a teacher or invigilator in the room to ask for help, but online who can help? In some cases there will be someone present, either live or virtually, as this may be a test used within a normal seminar time so you can inform your lecturer that the technology is not working. If there is not someone present, then you will need to contact your lecturer or the assessment coordinator as soon as possible. The important thing in this case is transparency and timeliness. If you come across a technical problem part of the way through the assessment and email or phone for support immediately, there will be a record of this contact and it can be used as proof that there was an issue. If you do not inform anyone until after the exam is complete, then there is very little someone can do to fix the problem in the moment. There could be doubts about whether you tried to complete the exam or just failed to turn up.

> ONLINE
> HURDLE
>
> Technological barriers are the biggest hurdle to overcome when sitting an online multiple-choice exam. These exams can include video or audio clips as well as several pages of questions with tick boxes. This is quite a complicated viewing page and can look different on different devices. Check with your assessment coordinator or lecturer which devices are compatible with the exam format.

As we all know, things can go wrong when using unfamiliar technology, particularly when you may be feeling more anxious than normal, so if you accidentally submit the assessment before you have finished it, for example, or indeed if anything goes wrong, the best thing to do is contact whomever you have identified in advance as your 'go-to' person or team on the day. It may be that they can open up the assessment again. In the case of a video link that can only be activated once, quite often the assessment coordinator or exams officer has an administrator's link to access the same material so it may be that they can give you access via this route, allowing you to complete your assessment.

ONLINE
BENEFIT

Prior to the exam, when preparing for the assessment, peer groups can be really helpful in supporting the revision process, and these are easy to set up online. Having a study buddy who you can share resources with and who can help motivate you is a good way to keep yourself on schedule for your revision, helping you feel more prepared for the exam.

How should I prepare?

Finding out the practicalities two weeks in advance gives you time to practise mock assessments prior to the assessment although, obviously, you will need to find out what material is covered earlier than this so that you can revise.

Once you know what the exam will entail and when it will be set then you can start planning your environment. Although anxiety might be lessened due to completing the exam at home do not be lulled into a falsely relaxed state; this is still an exam and still needs you to be absolutely focused. In this vein, make sure that you create a quiet and private space to complete the assessment.

What do I do on the day?

On the day of the exam, it is worth checking that you have the relevant link and that your exam space is set up, informing other members of the household that you will need to have sole access to the WiFi during your exam time and that you are not to be disturbed. Having other devices using the WiFi can severely slow down your access to the exam material particularly if there is a video or audio clip you need to open.

If you cannot ensure that no other devices are using your WiFi during this time you could invest in a dongle that allows only your device to use that WiFi. If you have poor signal strength, then it may be a worthwhile investment if you will be needing to access online material on a regular basis. You can also increase your data allowance or use your phone as a hotspot. Not only reduce the online traffic in your learning environment but also reduce the real traffic by closing the door and asking your housemates to keep the noise down. If it is not possible to optimise your online access or reduce the noise in your house, then make sure you find a quiet space prior to the assessment day where you can access the assessment in peace.

Once you have checked that everything is working then you can get on with your day and do not need to think about the exam until about half an hour before.

In this half an hour make sure you have a bottled drink near your workstation, although not close enough to spill, and that you are ready for your exam. Mentally and physically prepare yourself as there is nothing quite as distracting as realising you need a break halfway through your exam or rushing from a heated debate with a family member straight into an exam.

Make sure that you have paper and a pen next to you as you may wish to make notes during the exam. In some cases, such as when you are expected to watch a video and then answer questions on it, you may wish to write reminders to yourself whilst you are watching. An example of this is in a British Sign Language receptive assessment where the candidate is asked to watch a five-minute clip in total, then watch the same clip broken down into four sections with three questions after each section. There are quite often names and numbers that are in the story and the multiple-choice answers may be very similar, for example, John, Jamil, Jia and Jimmy. It is useful in this case to have written down any letters you may have seen even if you did not catch the full name. When you see the possible answers, you can surmise that you must have seen Jimmy as you saw a J and a Y. If you are given the choice of checking your answers at the end of the assessment, these notes are also useful as well as noting down what the multiple choices were so you can double-check you ticked the right box.

How do I get higher marks?

As with any exam it is worth looking at the marking criteria early on in your revision process as you may find there is weighted marking, meaning some elements are given more potential marks than others. In the case of language learning it may be that being able to turn-take is weighted lower than correct pronunciation in a conversation exam, for example. Once you know the weighting and the criteria you will be able to revise accordingly, spending the majority of the time on the areas that will get you the higher marks.

Top tip

Read the criteria carefully and be specific in what you need to revise. Check with your lecturer if you are unclear about anything.

Follow the instructions minutely. If you do not grasp that you will only be able to watch a clip once, then you will be panicked and unprepared when it will not let you play it again. With multiple-choice questions, some of them ask for you to tick one box whereas other questions will ask you to tick two, three or more boxes. A good way to reassure yourself that slowing down is acceptable is by working out how long you have to complete the exam and how many questions will be asked. Knowing this means you can work out how many minutes you get per question, and you will undoubtedly find that you have more time than you will need. This can help you relax and take your time. Work out the timings prior to the exam.

> ONLINE
> HURDLE

In an online exam, nerves about working online can affect the way you read through questions, making you skim through for the important words as opposed to reading through the whole question. Slow yourself down and read through everything, properly.

Understand the purpose of the exam and whether it is a formative or summative assessment; will these marks count towards a future grade? Of course each exam is important but recognising its relevance to your wider learning and qualification will help to put it into perspective, which can reduce anxiety and allow you to prioritise your revision time if you have several assessments for which you are preparing.

The more you prepare and revise for an exam the more you will build your confidence, making you more likely to approach the exam with a clear focus and make fewer mistakes. Preparation in the form of revision and preparation for working online are both important in completing online assessments.

What do students think?

Student quote

'I found completing an online exam from home much less scary once I had worked out how to access it. It was easier than I had expected!'

Some students were pleased to be sitting the exam at home as they could set up their environment in a reassuring way and they found that taking charge of the space and how they accessed the exam reduced anxiety. Other students felt that the additional responsibility for logging on and setting up their space was an extra stress.

Most students found that preparation in knowing what the exam would look like and how to access it was key to a successful experience with online assessment.

Many students felt that peer support was valuable when preparing for their exams. This came in many forms including a study buddy, someone to verbally test you on the material and a resource base such as sending links to revision tests or material via WhatsApp or on a private Facebook group. When sharing mock assessments or material which you may feel is dubious in its usefulness it is worth checking it with your lecturer; this means you will not waste your time looking at irrelevant material and nor will you share it with others.

Moving ahead

Once the exam has been completed it is worth taking the time to reflect upon your experience. Consider what made you nervous and what you would do differently next time, but also make a note of what went well as this is equally valuable in learning how to approach future online learning and assessments.

When moving ahead with your studies it is worth having a strategy for how your experience can help you in future. Multiple-choice tests can often give you a very clear indication of what you need to learn or revise and what you already know, which gives you a valuable insight into where to go next in both your study journey and your next stage of revision. Lecturers sometimes use multiple-choice tests to show where to go next with a group in terms of their teaching focus; you can make the most of the opportunity in a similar way. That way, you are working towards higher marks in any form of assessment in that topic area: a win–win situation!

7

Online short-answer tests

These tests can come at any time during your course and have multiple uses, which will be explored throughout this chapter. Online versions of this test format offer more options, giving you more scope to shine. In this chapter we will show you how to approach this challenge.

What is an online short-answer test designed to show?

An online short-answer test is designed to show your knowledge and understanding of the subject you are studying. If used at the beginning of a course, they might be an initial assessment to establish what you already know and what you still need to learn. In the middle of your course, they might be an informal class quiz or test that is either self-assessed or peer-assessed. Equally, you might find this used as a formative assessment to help you and your lecturer identify if there are gaps in your knowledge and understanding. A short-answer test may be part of your summative assessment too.

Skills

In these tests you will be expected to demonstrate your skills in terms of being clear, concise and correct. By recognising which questions are worth more marks, you can plan your assessment time to manage how much you will write for each answer. Being concise in your answers is a skill that may require some practice. It is an important skill for your studies and beyond, as being able to communicate in this way will have far-reaching benefits, in both the workplace and your ongoing learning.

The skills you demonstrate in a short-answer test are the same skills that you will be developing in preparation for exams. The following skills will be important to your overall success in this type of assessment:

- Writing concisely
- Answering questions with precision
- Producing high quality answers
- Drawing together multiple pieces of information
- Responding directly to the question

These will be covered in more detail throughout the rest of this chapter.

Knowledge

This type of test could happen at any stage of the term/academic year. If this assessment occurs at the start of the module or course that you are undertaking it will most probably be an initial assessment: a moment to recognise what you already know, allowing you and your lecturer to identify your starting point. You might have one or several short-answer tests throughout the year. Sometimes they are peer-assessed or self-assessed, meaning that they are marked against assessment criteria or prescribed answers by yourself or other students.

LECTURER'S
VIEW

We have found that short-answer tests early on in the module/course are useful as they show us what you and your class group already know and where the gaps are in your overall learning in an area.

Your subject knowledge will, of course, be under scrutiny but so will your presentation of the material. A short-answer test is time-restricted and there is limited space for writing. It is worthwhile looking at past papers and exemplars offered to you by your lecturers. Unless you are told otherwise, avoid using bullet points or lists. Unlike in exams, you probably will not need or have the time for extensive planning, but you may jot down a few key words (names, dates, subject-specific terminology) that you want to remember during your first read-through of the questions, or a brief overview note of what you will include in an answer.

What is involved?

Once logged in, you will be expected to complete the test within a set amount of time. If you have any queries or concerns, you should try to raise these with your lecturer before you start and preferably before the session. Once you have completed the test, you will need to submit it or, perhaps, upload it.

You should find out how you will receive the short-answer test paper: through your Virtual Learning Environment (VLE), via an emailed Word document, or through a separate assessment platform. Once you know this, you can then make sure that you are prepared for what you will see.

Top tip

Do not forget that logging onto online systems can sometimes take a bit of time and it is better to be in the online session early, rather than rushing in late and stressed.

Familiarise yourself with the online versions of tests to get yourself into the habit of planning and writing excellent short answers. Typing and working online are different to handwriting in a paper-based test, so practising is a sensible idea.

Top tip

Short-answer tests require you to produce clear, concise and correct answers. Practising how you will answer these sorts of questions will greatly improve your chances of success.

How is the online version different?

An unintended consequence of having this type of test online is that it makes the word count equal among all students. In the paper-based version, students with smaller handwriting could write more in the text boxes and those with larger handwriting would write a bit less. Some online short-answer tests might include expanding text boxes but if they do not, then the word count is automatically capped. The online version of this test has challenges and benefits, which we will consider here.

What challenges might this bring?

Online short-answer tests do have some challenges. By recognising them here, you can work to overcome them. For example, it can feel more difficult to see an overview of the whole test, whereas, with a paper copy, you would be able to flip back and forth between the pages and questions quickly and easily. It is a sensible idea to read through all the questions in the first instance so that you can start thinking about your answers. In a class-based test you are likely to be able to plan your answers on a piece of rough paper that you might then attach to the test paper. This is not possible in an online test, so you should have paper and pen ready, or a blank document open, in case you would like to make any notes or plans. With a short-answer test, your plan is unlikely to be extensive and may be just a few key dates, names or words that will prompt you as you go along.

Top tip

A 10-mark question will require you to give more detail than a 5-mark question. Try to find clear and distinct points for the answers in your online short-answer test.

In a short-answer test, you are expected to be concise, and people often find typing to be faster than handwriting, so there could be a risk that you write too much. By thinking before you type so that you are clear on the exact points you want to make, you will be able to mitigate this risk.

ONLINE
HURDLE

There is the risk that you over-type, delete and then regret deleting. With a handwritten answer you can still see through the crossing out and so can rewrite it if you decide you made a mistake. Do not delete unless you are certain you have the correct answer written and no longer need the information you initially typed.

Are there benefits to me with the online version?

There are, of course, benefits to completing short-answer tests online. For example, some students find it less distracting and nerve-wracking to be in a very familiar space. Although some nerves can be helpful, too much anxiety can be crippling. Having ready access to drinks and snacks during an assessment can be beneficial. It may seem basic but be sure that you are not hungry, thirsty, too cold or hot, uncomfortable or too tired to focus before you start your assessment. These things can make a difference when it comes to learning and assessment because if you are physically uncomfortable, your brain will be distracted by that when you want it to concentrate on the assessment.

The online version of this type of test offers you the chance to delete, copy and paste, so you can easily edit your answers. It might be that you have written too much under one question and that some of the material is more relevant to another question, so you can move it. Online short-answer tests are especially useful to you if you are uncertain about completing online assessments, as you can familiarise yourself with the format.

Online tests can offer a greater degree of anonymity as nobody will be seeing your handwriting. Although anonymous short-answer tests can be orchestrated for on-campus assessments, it is something that might be used more often online as it is easy to set up.

Top tip

By taking a screenshot of online short-answer tests or quizzes that you complete online, you will have a record of the sort of questions that could come up in later assessments. This will give you the chance to rework your answers as practice. You could store these in a single named file so that they are easy to find when you come to revising.

What do I need to know?

With online assessments, as with on-campus assessments, there is a process by which they will be marked, and this will depend on whether it is a formative test, a class quiz or a whole-module test. If the test is a formative one, then it will not have the same marking process as a summative assessment in terms of being seen by an external examiner. You might receive either a mark or some feedback if this is a formative test. If it is a class quiz or a self- or peer-assessed test, you might not receive feedback as it is simply designed to help you practise writing for the formative and summative assessments.

Top tip

> If you have received feedback on an assessment that you do not understand, try to respond to the person giving you feedback promptly as it can be difficult for them to remember the details of your answers if weeks have passed since they last saw it.

Short-answer tests allow enough space for you to share your ideas without feeling the pressure of writing long answers. The answers you will write are snippets of your total knowledge and these bite-sized chunks will come together to form longer answers in summative assessments later. By practising the format of short-answer questions, you are preparing for writing longer answers.

If these online short-answer tests are in the form of quick quizzes during seminar or class time, they may be found at the start, middle or end of sessions and they each have a different purpose. If used at the start of the session, the quiz will be a tool for reminding you of what you already know, getting you to focus on the session ahead and for flagging up to your lecturer any common areas that need developing. A mid-session quiz is a good way of summarising a topic and you should try to keep a copy of it for revision purposes. If the quiz comes at the end of a class, it is likely to be a way to ascertain how much of what has been taught has been understood and remembered by the cohort, and it will help you to condense and remember new knowledge.

Top tip

> Some VLE sites will have a statistics tracking feature, whereby we can see who has accessed what and for how long. Your short-answer test may be time-restricted but if it is not, do be aware that the amount of time you are spending on it might be seen by your lecturers.

Where do I go for help?

Although you might go to your lecturer to seek help in the first instance, you should also consider who else might be able to help you. For example, your academic or personal tutor, your mentor, your study support service or a study buddy from the year group above you. Be cautious if you are asking a peer to help you as they may not have the correct information. However, if there is a topic that several students need revision on in class, your lecturer might be able to make room for it in a future session, so letting them know is a good idea.

The library staff will have a treasure trove of information to share and will be able to signpost you to useful resources. Utilising your study support service may be an option to consider if you struggle with these assessments as there you will be offered personalised advice.

ONLINE
HURDLE

It can feel difficult to source help when you are not studying on campus, and you can begin to feel isolated and anxious, particularly around assessment time. By joining or forming online student groups, you will feel more connected to your peer group and your learning experience.

Peers who are studying alongside you will be useful as study buddies and we find that many class groups keep in contact through WhatsApp and other social media channels. For those late-night questions, it is helpful to be able to talk with other students. Check if the department you are studying in has a system of support between year groups, as you may also find that useful.

Subject-specific online communities are worth looking into, particularly for postgraduate students. These are an excellent source of information for your research as well as a brilliant way of connecting with like-minded people who could become part of your network for future research and employment opportunities.

How should I prepare?

There are so many different platforms and formats for online short-answer tests, and it would be wonderful if all universities chose just one for all academics to use. However, this is not the case, and each university will find what works best for its students and staff. Before beginning an online short-answer test, find answers to these questions:

- What is its purpose?
- Is it anonymous?
- Is it recorded?
- Is it formative or summative?
- Will there be feedback?
- Who else will see the answers?
- Do the marks go towards your final grade?

Generally, you can expect to be given this information during the introduction to the test. If you are unsure about anything, do ask. It might be that you can ask through an online chat function.

There are several things you can do to prepare for an online short-answer test. You could use the 'to-do' tick list below to ensure that you are ready to impress in your upcoming test.

What to do to prepare for an online short-answer test

✓ Revise class notes – abbreviate them to smaller chunks of information.

✓ Use flash cards/posters/other resources to revise.

✓ Test yourself (either with help from a study buddy or by writing out questions on one side of a card and the answers on the back).

✓ Complete mock assessments online if there is the chance to do so.

✓ Look at sample short-answer tests if they are available, such as past papers.

✓ Reflect on the areas that you are struggling with and focus on those.

✓ Teach someone else the information you need to know (teaching really is a very good way of learning and committing information to memory).

Preparation for these short-answer tests will mainly be from your own course notes, resources such as handouts, recorded lectures and recommended websites, and interactions with your peers. Your course notes are the key to excellent preparation for online short-answer tests or quizzes. When you write down (in any form – lists, full sentences, spider diagrams and the like) information that you are learning, it helps you to deepen your understanding of it and strengthen the connections within your memory. Continued revision of specific information will move it to your long-term memory.

There have been studies showing that reading handwritten notes aids learning and retention better than typed notes, so you may want to consider writing out flash cards, revision posters and class notes. In terms of preparing to undertake these tests online, you should not just have handwritten notes but practise typing your answers. Knowing what your online short-answer test will look like is useful and so browsing the platform that will be used is a sensible thing to do before your test.

The best way of being prepared for short-answer tests is to be organised and proactive. When you have completed a class session, make sure that you have made useful notes (do not be tempted to type up everything or record what you already know as this is likely to be a waste of time) and make sure that they are organised. When you have breaks in your schedule, take the time to condense your notes into a revisable format. Online short-answer tests or quizzes through the module will give you an insight as to what it is you really need to work on in preparation for your summative assessment.

It may seem old-fashioned in an education system that is becoming ever more digitalised, but a study buddy can be of great value to you. This is someone whom you can utilise to make sure that you get class notes should you miss a session, they are someone you can ask about elements of your studies that you are struggling with, and you can quiz each other in preparation for assessments. There is a saying by philosopher Xun Kuang (date unknown, translated by Dubs, 1928: 113[1]): 'Tell me and I forget. Teach me and I remember. Involve me and I learn.' Even if your peer knows the topic very well, have a go at teaching them and you will find that the information is more firmly fixed in your mind as you have thoroughly engaged with the course content. If you have access to the software, create short-answer tests for each other so that you get used to the format.

Top tip

If you know that you will be asked to use a particular software, download it during this preparation time so that you are not held up when it comes time for your assessment.

Practise writing answers to the questions that are likely to come up in short-answer tests. You may come up with the questions yourself based on what you already know, you could find them on your VLE under your course area or they might be stored online in a past paper section of your institution's website. If you are accessing these sorts of websites, check their validity as there are many websites that offer misinformation to students. You might find that your reading list includes useful websites, your lecturer could signpost you to them or you might find them and assess if you think they are good websites.

---

[1]Dubs, H.H. (translator) (1928) *The Works of Hsüntze, Book 8: The Merit of the Confucian*. London: Arthur Probsthain.

What should I do on the day?

ONLINE
BENEFIT

A significant benefit of completing this type of assessment online is that you do not have to physically go to a test, which might mean that you are less nervous when the time comes to undertake it.

On the day of your short-answer test, make sure that you have set up your workspace so that you are not going to be distracted or disrupted. Turn your phone onto silent and put it out of sight, turn off social media notifications on the computer and shut down any other documents or websites that you have been using. You should check that you can see the screen clearly and that you are comfortable; this might seem obvious but working under stress with glare on your screen or in an uncomfortable typing position can be surprisingly damaging.

Make sure that you give yourself time before the test to check through your revision notes and to log in. The process of getting into an online classroom or assessment can be slow, particularly if your internet connection is not great, so allow time for this. To prevent your technology from being a hurdle to completing an online assessment, ensure that your device has had all its updates well in advance. To limit disruptions, tell your household that you will be sitting a test.

You should follow to the letter the instructions that you are given at the start of the test. There is a reason that a test has been put together in a particular way (timings, with or without access to notes, mark weighting) and so you should stick to the directions given. This way, your results will be a genuine reflection of your abilities within that assessment format.

In an on-campus assessment, you might find the conversations with peers framing the test a comfort. There is something reassuring about sharing the experience, even if you are not particularly nervous or anxious about it. Online learning can make you feel isolated from other students, which can increase anxiety and related mental health conditions.

Students who would usually rely on peer contact may find tests, even informal quizzes, to be very stressful. Some lecturers, universities and students' groups have identified and responded to this by establishing online class groups, social groups and virtual support networks. If at any point you begin to feel isolated or anxious, you could seek support through these groups. If it begins to have a negative impact on coursework and tests, inform your personal tutor and the lecturers who are expecting work from you so that they are aware of the situation and can signpost you to groups and additional support.

One of the drawbacks of online tests is being too comfortable. It might be expected that students undertaking a test in their pyjamas will not be as alert and engaged as if they were properly dressed and prepared for going into a classroom or lecture hall. Although course assessments are not designed to test physical capabilities, physical preparedness is essential when it comes to learning and assessment. If your body has not been woken up properly then your mind will not be ready to focus. Getting a little bit nervous can be a good thing before any assessment as it gets the adrenaline going, ensuring that your mind is alert and ready to deal with stressful situations.

How do I get higher marks?

The key things you need to do to achieve higher marks are to be clear, concise and correct. To give the correct answers you simply need to revise, memorise and internalise. We say 'simply' as, although it can feel arduous, it is a basic and logical process. Your memory requires repetition of information as well as a true understanding of it to be able to recall it. The move from your short-term memory to your long-term memory is something that you can facilitate through not just trying to memorise individual modules of information, but by breaking down and building up again the meaning of that information. Our brains work through a series of associations, and by connecting the course material with previously embedded knowledge, you are far more likely to be able to retain and recall facts.

The other two challenges – being concise and clear – are things that you can practise. Once the information is firmly settled and can be recalled with ease, it is time to practise how to represent that information online. You should rehearse this in the same way that you would practise riding a bike – you try the same sort of thing in multiple ways/situations to be sure that you are confident in doing it. Setting up practice tests online will help you prepare to get higher marks.

If you have trouble being concise, type your answer and then highlight the key points you have made, and only those key points. Now look at what you have on the page. How much of it is necessary? You do not want to shorten your sentences to bullet points, but you also do not need your answers to be as elaborate as you might have originally made them.

ONLINE
BENEFIT

Your typed answers to practice questions can be easily stored and reviewed when you come to revise for later assessments. If you have received feedback on your answers, make notes if corrections are needed before you save the document so that you have accurate revision notes to rely on.

What do students think?

Student quote

'I find these tests less stressful because it is quite quick to answer each question and it's not part of my final grade.'

There is a lot to recommend short-answer tests at the formative stage; they require you to think quickly and cannot demand too much in-depth evaluation or analysis. You might prefer these types of test questions as you do not have to focus for too long on each question, allowing a bit of a break for your brain after each is completed.

Short-answer class tests can feel informal and be very helpful to you, which can make them a positive experience. To make the most of them, you should keep a record (download and save or take screenshots) of these sorts of class tests so that you can go back at a later point. If you have received detailed feedback on one of your answers, go back and rewrite it based on the feedback so that you can practise being clear, concise and correct.

Moving ahead

Short-answer tests are useful to help you prepare succinct revision notes for your summative assessments, they help you to focus your knowledge into short answers and short-answer tests are a flexible and varied assessment format. Being able to write concisely is something that will stand you in good stead for writing your CV and covering letter. It will also give you the chance to practise how to funnel your wider knowledge into a brief summary, which is a useful skill for most careers.

8

Online exams

For many students, the idea of an online exam was completely unfamiliar until recent times, so it is not surprising that this type of assessment causes anxiety. That is why, in this chapter, we are going to take you back to the basics, thinking with you about the purpose of exams and what you, and your lecturers, are trying to achieve. We also want to show you what you can take from your previous experience of traditional, on-campus exams, so that you do not feel that you are having to learn a whole new skillset. Of all the forms of online assessment, exams are probably the easiest for transferring your existing techniques, even though they often seem the most daunting.

As a student said to us very recently: 'I wish I had not wasted so much energy worrying about them – online exams suit me fine.' This is the experience of many of our students: it feels unfamiliar to take an exam online, and students become understandably concerned about how much support they might be losing. In fact, they usually find that online exams suit them very well, but only when they have got used to the idea and mastered some of the techniques that we are sharing with you here.

What is an online exam designed to show?

Skills

Luckily, an online exam is used to show the same skills as any exam, even though you might face some new challenges in how you demonstrate those skills. The skills that you will need to develop for success in exams are:

- Being able to demonstrate your wider understanding
- Good judgement in your selection of exam questions and the information you choose to use in responding to them
- Time management
- Management of material

Wider understanding

Whilst a focused class discussion or essay can show your knowledge in a specific area of your studying, an exam often requires far less depth of knowledge than, say, an extended piece of coursework. The fact that an online exam might be 'open' for you to work on it longer than if you had been sitting in an exam hall does not mean that you are now expected to have a vast store of knowledge that you would not have had before.

LECTURER'S VIEW

Although we know that much of what makes students nervous about exams is not knowing what questions will be asked, as lecturers we know that this is actually a benefit to those students who have worked on their exam technique. You have to think on your feet, but this is a skill that you can acquire, and success in exams is about using your knowledge under pressure.

The key to success is the word 'understanding' in the heading of this section. Exams are about what you know – of course they are – but they are far more about how you use what you know. Often those students who do well in exams are not those who revise for the longest time, or cram the greatest number of facts into their brains; they are the students who understand how exams work and who practise using their knowledge by taking an active approach to revision.

Judgement

There are two main demands on your judgement in an exam – can you choose the questions that show off your knowledge and arguments to best effect, and can you master the material in such a way that it impresses the person who is marking your exam? If you can do both of these things, then you will gain the most marks for your knowledge (what you know) and your arguments and application (how you use what you know). This judgement comes with practice, but you can lose track of some of your exam techniques when you are faced with an online exam. The easiest way to remove this danger is to make sure that some of your revising takes place online, so that it becomes a comfortable place for you in the context of exams.

Top tip

> Taking mock exams online is especially helpful, because then you can say to yourself that you really know what the real exam will feel like.

Use of time

This is perhaps the single most worrisome aspect of online exams for most students. Your university will decide how much online time you are given for an exam, but then you have to decide how much time you actually spend on the exam. This is such a challenging area that we have included several case studies later in the chapter to help you decide on your approach.

ONLINE HURDLE

If your exam is more like a class test (an exam-like situation that would usually happen in the classroom, be relatively brief – perhaps just an hour – and might take place several times a term) you might expect that our more online world nowadays would not have much effect, but you could be wrong. Whilst students in different time zones or with differing family circumstances can all access the same pre-recorded material easily enough, a test might need to run for many hours if students are expected to do the test online. So, what was a simple hour-long event on campus might become a far more protracted process online.

Use of material

It is worth repeating that exam success is about making good use of your material, rather than simply remembering masses of facts or training your brain to recall huge swathes of material. This should be good news – less time spent monotonously trying to force yourself to remember things – but it can also be daunting. A live exam that takes place in a hall for a set amount of time works to a straightforward formula:

I revise so that I understand things better and remember material

+ I attend an exam with set questions that are designed to draw out my understanding and material recall

+ I revised with a similar set of questions in mind

+ I have a limited amount of time within which to do this, a time set by the examiners

= if I play it right, exam success follows.

There are several features that you might notice about this formula. The first is that it will feel very familiar to you, because you have been taking exams, in one form or another, for years (which also means that you might feel fairly confident about your abilities in this area). The second point of note is that it is a very set formula – most exams you have ever taken will have worked within this formula. The questions might have been multiple choice, and the time you were given might have varied a little with the length or number of answers that were expected of you, but generally this formula will have been followed.

The last aspect of this formula you might notice is that your role in it is largely passive. Other people are setting the questions, as other people have always set the questions, and you have been told how long you can have to answer those questions, usually whilst someone is watching you do this. The only chance for you to be active is in the way you revise (more on this later) and in the limited choice you are given (if any) over which questions to answer.

LECTURER'S VIEW

Students sometimes assume they are not very clever or not very brave if they prefer coursework assessment to exams. In our experience, it is often more a case of being active: students who excel in coursework take an active approach to their assignments and take control of the situation. So, you need never feel bad if you are not a fan of exams!

If you are asked to take a familiar sort of exam, perhaps for two or three hours, and it is at a set time and day and you simply have to work online as if you were in an exam hall, you might not find the experience too strange. However, elements within the exam will be different, as you will have access to far more material than in an exam room, and you will feel responsible for accessing the exam site. You might also find that typing rather than hand writing your exam answers, if this is unfamiliar to you, will alter the amount and nature of the material you tend to include.

This chapter will deal with all of these issues, but it will also be based on the assumption that there is another, far more radical change to your exam experiences. Different home circumstances, along with time zone differences and the delays that technical glitches can cause, have led universities to explore the option of exams that last far longer usual – up to 24 hours would not be unexpected. As with all formulae, varying just a single element can alter everything. In an online exam, if the element of time is changed, this will distort everything else for you, to a greater or lesser extent.

Of course, it might be that you are used to 'pre-released exams' (sometimes called 'take-home exams') in some courses or modules, where you are given access to the questions before the exam day. You might also have experience of 'open-book exams', where you can take material into the exam room with you. Variations on exam structure such as these are used in some courses and for some students, but the idea of being given many hours to undertake an exam, by yourself and at a distance, is worryingly unfamiliar territory to most students.

The way this will affect your use of material is likely to be significant. No longer do you have to worry about not having memorised enough material before you go into an exam; now you have to get your head around having almost limitless material at your disposal, and this is going to require a new set of rather more active skills. In the rest of this chapter, we will take you through the path to success, stage by stage, helping you to overcome new hurdles and make the most of the opportunities that online exams can bring.

What is involved?

Although this is going to be a different sort of exam experience for you, some of the same traditions around exams will still apply. You will still need to revise, and you will still need to be ready to begin your exam, however long it is, with a good sense of the areas you would want to cover and many of the facts that you need to hand.

Preparing for revising

Although the mechanics of an online exam will differ from your past experience, the amount of material and knowledge you are bringing to that exam will be just the same, so you will still need to go back through the material you have produced during the year. Some of our students did not do this last year and found it impossible to excel in their exams because they simply did not have the knowledge, the synthesis of facts and ideas, that they needed in order to tackle the exam.

As one of them said to us: 'If only I had had 23 days rather than 23 hours, I might have stood a chance!'

The reality of online exams is that, although you will have the chance to access far more material during the exam, you will still spend time revising. However, that time will be redirected towards making sure that you are not overwhelmed with material, or easily lost within each question, on the day of the exam.

Every student has a slightly different revision method, so we do not plan to completely overhaul your existing routine here, but it is worth stressing that working through your notes is going to be vital. However, rather than highlighting points you want to remember, you can take a slightly easier and more active approach. For each set of your notes (that is, notes you took in a lecture or seminar or other learning events, along with notes that you made from your reading, practical work or lab sessions) you can challenge yourself to extract from them only the most important material. This will comprise facts, theories and ideas.

Once you have reduced your notes in this way (and this is going to take up a significant amount of your overall revision time for an online exam, so you need not stint on it) you can leave them alone for a while, letting what you have read during the process settle in your mind. A little time later, go back to those reduced notes and highlight the pieces of material that, on reflection, you think are most important. By now, your notes should look very different from when you started. Depending on the density of the original material, it would not be surprising to find that you now have notes that are perhaps one quarter to one fifth of the length of your original notes.

You may not find it easy to reduce your notes, and this need not be a worry. If it does not come naturally to you to cut out the less relevant parts of your material, you can go through your notes three or four times, reducing little by little as you go. Remember, each time you do this you are deepening your understanding and retaining more information. Revising can be a beneficial learning experience.

ONLINE
BENEFIT

There is a HUGE advantage to online exams during this stage of your revision. For a live exam you might expect to be testing yourself over and over to see if you can remember your reduced notes and then cutting out the material you can recall, leaving behind a mass of material that you still have to remember. For online exams you still need to be able to recall things quickly, as you will not want to ruin your flow or your concentration by having to look up every single fact or idea, but you can reduce your notes to the point where they are a brilliant reference resource for you, without having to commit to memory every scrap of material you might want to use in the exam.

How your reduced notes will look tends to vary from student to student. Some like to highlight sections of their notes and then cut and paste those sentences when they are sure that they are the most important. Other students prefer to rewrite the most important points, bringing them together in short sentences or bullet-pointed lists. You may already have a preferred way to carry out this part of your revision, and the prospect of an online exam need not make you change your normal method at this stage.

Top tip

Notice that we are referring here to 'sentences' not 'sections'. At each stage your aim will be to make the briefest possible set of prompts, because you will not want to waste time in the exam reading pages and pages of rather undigested material. Instead, you want to be able to power ahead with what you want to say, with just a brief glance at your final set of reduced notes from time to time.

Remembering

If you are not keen on learning lists of facts by rote, simply repeating them or writing them down over and over again to make sure that they are drummed into your brain, then you are likely to welcome online exams as great news. If you are the sort of student who finds it fairly easy to recall quotations, facts and figures, you might well want to continue to develop this recall even for online exams. This is because, for you, a quotation or a recalled fact or formula is probably a springboard to your next ideas and argument in an exam, so you will not want to change your method too much – there would be no need.

LECTURER'S VIEW

Many academics are delighted by this aspect of online exams, believing that education should be more about developing and then using your knowledge than simply remembering data. This is one reason why online exams might become a more routine feature of the assessment landscape in future.

Just because you do not have to remember facts, figures and quotations, it still makes sense to spend time identifying which material you are most likely to need, so ensure that the reduced notes we described above include enough hard information to support you.

One complete run-through of a past paper or example exam with complete answers as if you were in the exam might be extremely useful for you if you feel nervous or unsure of your exam abilities. Beyond this, we would suggest answering multiple questions, as many as you have time for, but just in note form.

To do this, you would take a step-by-step approach:

- Choose a series of two to four questions that you want to try out as a mock exam (the number depends on how much time you have but more than four might leave you too tired to do yourself justice).
- Take the first question and make a plan for the answer you would want to give (there is more on how to do this in the 'What should I do on the day?' section of this chapter).
- Now expand your plan to show a bullet-pointed list of what you would want to include in each section of the plan.
- If there is an idea you know you would want to include, or a point of argument that you want to practise, you might include some full sentences in this expanded plan.
- At the end of the expanded plan, take one look back to make sure that the flow of your answer works and that, now you have a moment to reflect, you cannot spot anything obvious that you should have included.
- Resist the temptation to do any more to that answer and move onto the next, repeating the process until you have all the answers in front of you. Leave them alone for a while – ideally a few hours or overnight.

When you come to look at your exam answers again, you might see some errors, gaps in your argument or missing material. Now would be a good time to make a note of these points so that the answers become part of your resources for revision. You could leave it there, but there is one more step you can take to make the most of your mock exam. Go back through your revision notes and see if there are any details you would like to add.

Adding detail might lead you to realise that you have left out quite a lot of material that you should have included, and this realisation will be valuable to you: this is an area where you need to do more revision. If you find that there are small details you have left out (date, names, fact and figures, nice little quotes or references you might include) then by adding them in now you have a far more polished resource, one that will serve you very well as you move towards the exam.

You might ask why you need to add in any detail, given that the exam is online and so you could look at your notes at the time. The problem is, looking up material regularly when you are trying to sit an online exam can leave you flustered and exhausted, and it could well ruin the line of your argument or the logical flow of the process you are trying to describe or evaluate. It seems like a gift to be able to use material like this in an exam; it can often turn into a negative distraction.

Polishing your material and technique

What you are aiming to do as you revise for an online exam is to have a set of materials (reduced notes that you have made, some exam plans, some mock exams) that are polished enough to be useful, but not so polished that you cannot break the material down to repurpose it. A full and perfect practice answer to a question, however good it is, will be difficult to reuse unless you are asked exactly the right question – and the temptation to use it regardless of the fact that it does not quite answer the question will be overwhelming. In contrast, an answer that is in notes and bullet points, that contains plenty of material but is brief enough that you can see how to break it up for a new question – that is the perfect amount of polishing.

How is the online version different?

However nervous (or even downright scared) you might feel on the morning of an on-campus exam, you can comfort yourself with the knowledge that, by lunchtime, it will all be over. When supporters say 'just do your best' they really mean it, because once the two or three hours of the exam are over, there is nothing you can do to change the outcome. You revised, prepared and did your best for that brief period of exam time, and now you can relax and move on.

There are obvious ways in which an online exam will *feel* very different to an exam you undertake in an exam hall, alongside your fellow students and with an invigilator watching over you all. These differences should not be overlooked, and we will be returning to them when we consider how you might approach the day of the exam. Before that, though, there are two practical differences that cannot be avoided: you will have too much time, even if it does not feel like it, and you will certainly have access to way too much material.

What challenges might this bring?

You might be given plenty of guidance as to what your university expects, but there cannot really be any rules, as such. There also cannot be any easy technical fixes to this problem of your exam time. A university might, for example, try setting up an online exam space which cuts your access two or three hours after you log in, but that is not practical because you could have an internet failure, or any number of other interruptions, during that time. An institution might consider running a series of 'live online' exam events, starting, say, every three hours; this would solve the problem of time zones but not of other factors such as students having uninterrupted access to the internet whilst trying, for example, to take an exam in a busy home environment. So, we must assume that you could still be facing a lengthy exam time, far longer than you would be given in a live, on-campus exam.

Top tip

It is going to hinder your performance if you approach an online exam with no idea of how you will tackle it. You will need to have your exam technique firmly in your mind, and feel confident that it will work for you, before the exam day arrives.

Some of our students have been concerned about the ethics of a lengthy online exam slot. If they are advised to spend just two hours on an exam, despite having access to the material for far longer than that, is it cheating to work on it for many more hours? Would that give them an advantage that would make them feel bad about themselves? Would they be happy with their mark, knowing that they had spent so long obtaining it? If they were then awarded a lower than expected mark, would they be demoralised because they had spent so long on the exam? Perhaps the best way to answer these questions is to think practically about how you can approach the situation.

In Tables 8.1, 8.2 and 8.3 you can see how an exam might look for three students. The first is prepared to stay awake and (maybe) alert for 23 hours and dedicate that time to an exam; the second plans to stick rigidly to the time that would have been allowed in an on-campus exam; the third takes a more nuanced approach to the situation.

Table 8.1   Online exam situation: case study 1

Case study 1	
Scenario	The student who works on the exam for the whole 23 hours period that is available.
How might it look?	Completely unrealistic! It would not be possible to work consistently and productively for 23 hours. You might be able to sit at your computer for that long, but there is no way your brain will work at optimal pace for all of those hours. Although you might have a good first six hours or so, after that you will be tired and finding it difficult to concentrate; after 12 hours you will be tweaking your work rather than adding anything much to it; after 18 hours you will be second-guessing everything you have done so far. By that point there is a danger that you will undo the good work you did in those early few hours.

(Continued)

Table 8.1 (Continued)

Case study 1

The advantages	You will be able to tell yourself that you have done your absolute best because you engaged with the exam for the longest possible time. Despite the warnings above, for students who are nervous about their ability in exams, this can be a huge temptation.
The disadvantages	You will not get any cleverer in that 23-hour period, so you will not improve your grade that way; more importantly, the exam questions were designed to produce enough material to give a good answer in a limited time. If you produce six times more words than the student who spent far less time than you, it would be illogical to expect that your quality will improve with more words. You will not be marked on how *much* material you can create, but on how well you can *use your* material in response to a question.

Top tip

If you are told only to produce answers of a certain number of words, you need to check whether the markers have been instructed to stop reading at around that set number. There is no point adding in hundreds, or even thousands, of extra words if nobody will be looking at them, and producing them might weaken earlier sections of your answers.

Table 8.2 Online exam situation: case study 2

Case study 2

Scenario	The student who sticks strictly to the two hours that has been suggested.
How might it look?	Very similar to a regular two-hour exam, but not quite the same. It takes a little time to settle into an exam that you are taking in an unusual exam setting. You will inevitably look at some brief material that you have prepared in advance (unless you have been told not to do this) and so it would be unlikely that you could achieve the same results in exactly the same amount of time.
The advantages	If you have several exams scheduled in a relatively short space of time, devoting just the set number of hours you would have had in a campus-based series of exams does mean that you will avoid exhaustion and you will have time to prepare well in advance for each exam. You will also keep the rhythm of a regular exam, so you will benefit from the familiarity of your usual exam technique.

Case study 2	
The disadvantages	You might panic about whether you have done enough, which could tempt you to keep going back to the exam in a rather haphazard way, but the main disadvantage revolves around marker expectations. If you are in an exam room and you have two or three hours to complete an exam, any marker will overlook the fact that you were unable to remember quite the right date for an event or the exact terminology for a process. For an online exam of many hours, a marker might expect that you could quickly look up that date or check out the correct term.

Table 8.3   Online exam situation: case study 3

Case study 3	
Scenario	The student who takes a mixed approach.
	(This is our favoured approach to how students can make the most of the time in a lengthy online exam slot, so we are going to share it with you in some depth.)
How might it look?	Ideally, you will set up an 'exam room' – a space where you can sit at your computer undisturbed, knowing that you can take a break, grab a snack or have a walk. Unless you have been clearly instructed to take a certain approach to the timing and conduct of the exam, you can decide in advance how much time you would want to spend working on it. You go into the exam room at the point when you are ready to work on it (so no sneak peeking as soon as it is released) and you will begin as for an on-campus, timed exam – we will help you with techniques for that later in this chapter.
	Once you have reached a stage where you are happy to take a break (this might be when all, or just one of your answers is planned out) make sure that you leave the room for a short while. It is important that you take a proper break: even if it is just for a few minutes, moving away from the space will help you to reset your brain. You will have decided whether you prefer to plan each answer and then write it before turning to the next question, or whether you would rather complete all of your planning before you write anything, so you will know when this planning break – or series of breaks – should happen.
	In a timed, on-campus exam, you would need to start writing as soon as you had reached this point, but we are suggesting more than just a break to rest your brain for a moment. One major advantage of an online exam is that you do have material *that you have prepared in advance* that you can use in the exam. Now is the time to look back through it so that you can make some quick but firm decisions about what to include, and you can also confirm to yourself that your plan will work. What you will not need to do now is to trawl back through lecture notes or notes you have made during your research. Your revision will have made this unnecessary – that is why you revised even though your exams are online.

(Continued)

Table 8.3   (Continued)

Case study 3	
	Your refusal to let yourself look back through thousands of words of notes and thoughts, your determination to look only at your revision notes and mock exams at this stage, is not about timing; after all, you have hours at your disposal. It is about clarity and cleverness. If you want to show off how well you have learnt the material on your course, how well you understand the concepts and arguments in your subject area, the smart move is not to muddy the waters by confusing yourself at this moment. You have made plans, you have taken a break to reflect on their validity and you have spent some time adding in material to strengthen them. Now, just write.
	But for how long? This is another significant gain with an online exam. If you tire easily when you write, you can take a break between answers, which will help you perform at your best. However, we would urge you to think twice before taking a break – or series of breaks – *during* the writing of each answer. If you feel yourself getting muddled or uncertain, a minute or so staying in your exam room but looking about and resting your eyes (and your brain) should be enough to get you back on track. Taking longer breaks than that during the production of each answer is likely to derail your train of thought and make you more tired by the end of the exam.
	When you have completed an answer (or perhaps all of the answers, if that is what you have decided in advance would work best for you) spend no more than 10–15 minutes reading them through, just to make sure that you have not made any blunders, that you have actually answered the questions that were asked and that it all looks as you expect. Then, take a decent break (an hour or so if you like, if the entire exam is complete now) and come back to the paper, rested and ready to do a final work-through.
	In this final stage you will not aim to add a large quantity of material, but you will be able to take advantage of the time you have to make any changes or add any material that you believe will make a significant difference to your mark. Once you have reached that stage, you are back to resisting temptation: this time, the temptation to keep reading your work to the point where you can no longer see just how good it is, and so might make poor choices about making changes.
The advantages	You will know that you have done your best, and probably rather better than you would have done in a shorter exam, but that you have not been tempted to tinker and perhaps reduce the impact of your answers. By the end of it you will be tired, but not utterly exhausted.
The disadvantages	The success of this approach relies on you being organised, planning your approach in advance and sticking to it even if you are nervous or facing a few questions that you had not expected.

As you will see from these case studies, your approach could vary widely from that taken by another student, so you might want to decide on your tactics before you share with others. This is because the way you face the exam is, to some extent at least, about the sort of person you are. If you are very anxious about exams, you could be tempted to give yourself the longest possible time undertaking the exam, although oddly enough, the reverse can be true. Extremely nervous students will sometimes become so anxious that they give themselves the least possible amount of time, scribbling out some answers before hastily turning off their computers.

If you are highly organised, or if you have revised thoroughly and given yourself many mock exams, you could be keen to give yourself just the two or three hours you would have had in a live, on-campus exam. You will be confident enough to do this, although you might miss the chance to have that final look through that can show that you need a little more work on your answers. However, if this is how you prefer to work you might be better off leaving those slight amendments rather than knocking your confidence, if you think taking some extra time could work against you.

The third approach outlined here is demanding. It requires you to prepare well and use your time wisely, to be confident in what you know and focus your energy on the best possible answer you can give, keeping up that discipline for a while longer than in a more limited, timed exam. It also necessitates knowing in advance how you will work through the exam.

Are there benefits to me with the online version?

Most of our students have responded positively to online exams, once they get used to the idea and are given clear guidance on what is expected of them. Here are some of the thoughts they have shared with us:

- They felt that you can use your revision time more productively. Although you still need to revise, rather than trying to memorise masses of material, you can make good sets of 'prompt notes' to help you in the exam and then spend your time working through your material to find good connections and persuasive arguments. All of the students we talked to said that they spent less time revising than usual, but most were still happy with what they achieved during revision.
- A couple of students found that they had over-revised compared to normal and had too much material ready for what was needed. One resented the wasted time, but the other said that it had stopped her getting too anxious before the exam, so she did not mind.
- Most students commented on the problems that they had encountered in the past with live on-campus exams. This included feeling ill during an exam but having to do it so

as not to have to face the whole process again later, or being so nervous that they were distracted from what they were trying to do, or domestic/social problems that had cropped up just before an exam that got in the way of concentration. For some of these students, the need to take an exam on a set day for a set amount of time meant that they underperformed, although some noted that, once the adrenaline kicked in, they were able to excel regardless.

LECTURER'S VIEW

We noticed that students recognised that they could achieve despite immediate difficulties because of the sense of occasion and urgency in an exam. When we talked this through, they asked us to pass on some advice: dress and sit for the exam as if you were in a live, on-campus exam so that you get your adrenaline going. Taking an exam from your bed in a onesie had been a disincentive for several of our students, who were surprised to find that they could think far better if they felt more like they were in an exam room.

- They all appreciated the extra time to look things up and to cope with any glitches – having time to read the exam paper multiple times without worrying that you were wasting too much time was highlighted as a very positive feature. However, most of the students were concerned about going back to on-campus, time-limited exams in future, worried that they might perform less well if they were back in that situation. They all agreed that mastering a firm set of exam techniques for online exams would help them with that transition, if it were to happen.
- We could all remember exams when we had looked at the clock and realised that we did not have enough time left to check through our answers. This was probably the online advantage that was mentioned most by our students. In general, they did not seem to want to use hours of extra writing time – they could see the dangers in that – but they were grateful for the time to proof-read thoroughly and check on their answers. This was not just about getting better marks – it was also about the satisfaction of knowing that they had done a good job and would not feel awkward about any errors they might have made because they were rushing.
- We were surprised to hear how lost some of our students felt after an on-campus, timed exam. For these students, their nerves might have helped them do well, but they had no clear sense of this once the exam was over. They said that often they could not really remember what they had written in the exam and so went around with an anxious feeling that they might have done badly, a feeling that could last until the exam results came out. For these students, online exams were a great benefit, allowing them time to relax a little before the end of the time allowed and see clearly that they really had done their best.

What do I need to know?

What you need to know before an online exam is simple:

- Access – how do you get to the exam and will it automatically save, or do you have to upload it?
- Rubric – the rubric is your set of instructions, and these are often released before the exam. They do not include the questions, but they give you valuable information such as how many questions you need to answer, how many areas or texts you need to cover and, perhaps, how the questions are divided between different sections of an exam.
- Time – how long do you have? Are you being advised to spend a certain amount of time on the exam regardless of the time that is available? You might choose how closely you follow this advice, but you do need to know if it exists.
- Materials – it is easy to assume that you will have access to anything you can find on the internet, but if you are asked specifically not to look at any external material during the exam, it makes little sense to do it. At best, you will have to work hard to fit this material into your answers; at worst you might be penalised for material that was clearly not generated prior to the exam.
- Length – are you being told to write answers of a certain length? Is this advice or a specific exam instruction? What will happen if you write an overlength answer?

Where do I go for help?

ONLINE
BENEFIT

One of the best aspects of more online learning is that your supporters are more likely to be available online to offer help when you need it. Rather than signing up to a face-to-face meeting, days or even weeks ahead, you could probably schedule an online support session quickly.

In the days and weeks before your exams you will access your usual sources of support as you prepare. It helps to know who is likely to be best placed to guide you in different aspects of your exam preparation, so here is a quick guide:

- Understanding – if you do not understand something from a single learning event (a lecture, a seminar or workshop, or a lab session, for example) it is usually best to go directly to the person who led that session, rather than the person who is leading a whole course or module (such as a module or course convenor).

- Making connections – if you are struggling as you revise, realising that you have not grasped some of the concepts, the course or module leader would be a good person to approach. At the very least you can expect that person to be able to remind you of the resources that would help make things clear for you.
- Remembering – if you have forgotten what some of your notes mean, or you are worried that you might have misunderstood something, you could try a revision group first, if you have one, or go back to other students who were working with you in a seminar or practical group, or who attended a lecture with you, to ask to compare notes. If you are left unsure at any point, and there are no reference resources to help you, always go back to your module or course leader.
- General – if you feel that something has passed you by, but you cannot pin down quite what is wrong, your personal or academic tutor is a good person to approach, as you can talk together to try to identify what help you need.
- Exam nerves – if you become very anxious about exams, your study advisors could be a good source of support, offering you extended help with exam technique They might also be able to put you in touch with your institution's wellbeing and/or counselling service.
- Technology – you will receive instructions of how to get help on the day of the exam if the technology at your university fails, and you will be given advice on what to do if your technology fails on the day. If your problem is that you have not mastered some software you could need, or you are not sure how the online exam system works at your university, your IT or learning technology department would be the best place to go.

ONLINE
BENEFIT

Before you wait in a queue to ask your technology question or spend too long trying to explain in an email what is wrong, make sure that you browse through all the many helpful guides and sets of instructions that will be available to you through your university and more widely online.

- On the day – if you need technical help during the exam, or you believe there is an error on the exam paper, you will be able to contact your university supporters (including, perhaps, your examinations office, your tutors and your IT and administrative teams). However, as these supporters will usually be working office hours, it makes sense to contact them during those hours, even if you do not plan to complete the exam until later.

How should I prepare?

The advice we offered on revision will help you in your general preparation for online exams, but there are two aspects of preparing in an online setting that are particularly worth considering.

Revision groups

If you know that you work best in a group and might benefit from the emotional support of a revision group, the online learning world is perfect for you. Rather than being restricted to face-to-face meetings or brief conversations after lectures or seminars, you can set up regular online meetings. You can also widen your revision group beyond your immediate study groups, perhaps to friends outside your university who are studying in a similar area, or to fellow students with whom you worked well in other settings.

One word of warning: if you are highly sociable you might find online interaction such as this a bit frustrating; you might prefer to schedule some face-to-face meetings if you can, so that you can enjoy all being in the same offline room.

If you are not used to working alone, you might want to try an online revision group – you might find that it works well for you. Whether or not you are inclined towards this type of group support, make sure that it continues to work well for you. Monitor how much revision you actually get through in each session so that you can decide whether it is worth your time. You can also make a social online group with the same people once the exams are over.

ONLINE
HURDLE

Although it can be easy to join an online revision group, it can be difficult to leave, especially if you feel that other members might be offended or see it as a personal slight. It makes sense to ask a trusted friend to recommend, or introduce you to, a revision group if you are concerned that this might happen to you.

Chat rooms

Chat rooms might be used for general studying and might morph into revision groups for a while before exams. If you are already chatting to fellow students online, you might want to suggest that some or all of the group set up some online sessions just for revising.

LECTURER'S
VIEW

We have set up some open study sessions for our students on our university Virtual Learning Environment (VLE) site. You could ask your lecturers to do this for you, too, so that you have some semi-formal space in which to revise together. We do not join the sessions unless our students ask us to, but we know they are used. Revision groups can go wrong very quickly, if false rumours start to circulate about the exams and how awful they will be, or if someone disagrees with the way someone else is approaching an exam. Having this more formal setting seems to reduce those dangers.

Subject specialist groups

We have been pleased to discover that some of our students, more used now to learning online, have joined up to specialist societies in areas they are studying. These are free and often give access to fascinating discussions amongst experts in a field of study. They might not give you a huge amount of material that will be directly relevant to your exams, but they could aid your understanding, boost your confidence and give you access to a few unusual resources for your exams.

External exam support groups

We have just typed 'exam help' into a search engine. The first 10 sites were exam cheat sites that offer to take your exam for you for money. We gave up looking at that point, not because there were not hundreds more on offer – there were – but because we know that anyone buying this book would not be interested in someone else taking their exam. However, if you ever are tempted it is worth pointing out two things: the exam they will be taking will not be your unique exam, it will be a version of an answer that they have cobbled together with an algorithm designed to give an approximate answer; also, your university will be ahead of the game on every one of these sites. You will get caught, and the punishments are startlingly severe.

What should I do on the day?

As soon as the exam is open for you to see it:

- You might naturally want to look through the paper in detail straight away but, as we suggested before, try to leave this in-depth perusal until you are at a point when you can give it enough thought to start planning your answers.

Top tip

> You may find that a 24-hour helpline or online live chat has been set up for students who get into technical difficulties. This is not something you want to be looking for during the exam, so find all of the details beforehand and note them down.

- You will still need to have a little look at the paper in office hours, though, just to make sure that you can access the correct paper and that there are no problems that you can see. If you notice anything wrong, call or email the invigilation (examination) team straight away so that you receive an answer to your query quickly.
- Make sure that your exam space offline is as ready as the online space. Ideally, you will find somewhere with few interruptions, with a drink and snack beside you.
- Read ALL the questions twice, even if you think you understand them. Misunderstanding a question is easy to do and comes with too high a price.
- Read the instructions, even if they were released before the exam and you had a look at them then. You will be looking in particular for instructions that affect the way you approach the exam. A multiple-choice exam might ask for answers in a certain order, a short-answer exam might want different word counts for different answers, a case study or experimental review answer might demand a particular layout.
- Even though you have material that you can access in your files easily, take a few minutes now to note down any stray points that spring into your mind as soon as you see the questions. Keep these little notes as brief as possible – notes not sentences, bullet points rather than fleshed-out thoughts.

ONLINE
BENEFIT

You can set up a document before the exam entitled 'exam thoughts' and have it ready for when you first look at the exam. That is where you put these stray thoughts. You might come back to them at various points – as you plan, when you get stuck for ideas, when your writing seems to be stalling – but most importantly you will check them at the end of your writing, to see if there are any impressive snippets you could add at that point.

- Jotting down some material like this will have cleared your mind, so now check the questions for the third time to confirm your choice as to which you plan to answer.
- Make a brief plan (no more than six main points, regardless of the intended length of your answer). This might be for all of your answers (giving you the chance to add to them every now and then as you are writing your earlier answers) or just for the first answer (keeping your mind clear to come afresh to the second answer).

Many years of experience have shown us that how you do this does not matter in terms of performance. Some students like to do all of their planning first; others like to plan and write and then plan and write again for the next answer. You do what feels right for you.

- Take a moment to think back to any mock exams you did; this should help to calm your nerves before the next stage.
- Look at the exam questions once more, just to be sure.
- Add material to your plan, making it detailed enough to write from and ensuring it shows a logical flow of impressive material and/or a strong and connected argument.
- Check back to your 'exam thoughts' document to see if you need to add anything more to the plan.

If you have a 'sticky note' program on your laptop, open it now. When little thoughts come to you during your exam writing, you need not be distracted – you can just jot them down on an onscreen sticky note.

- Take a good break away, as we suggested in case study 3 on p.119, and let your mind relax. Although you will not be consciously working, your brain will be processing, and you are likely to find useful ideas and connections bubbling to the surface. Note these down as they come to you ready for the writing stage.

ONLINE
HURDLE

Although it would feel logical to go back to your screen each time you want to jot down an idea, you might be better off with pen and paper or a phone to voice record your thoughts, so you do not find yourself back in the exam space before you are ready.

- Write your first answer. It sounds so simple, but we know it is not. You need to have decided in advance which answer to tackle first – the one that makes you feel confident because it is very familiar territory, or the one that is more challenging. The former will give you confidence ready for the other answers, but the latter would mean you face the most difficult answer when you are at your most energetic mentally. You will know which approach works for you, so trust your earlier decision on this.

Top tip

You will have noticed that most of the decisions being discussed here will have been made in advance of the exam. This is important because you will not want to make such important choices in the moment, and you will also find it reassuring to have decided what to do in advance: it will help you feel in control of the situation.

- Even though you may have many hours with your exam available, keep an eye on the time. If you begin to feel that you are taking so long on an answer that you are losing your way or will be too tired to write the next answer well, you could add a series of bullet points to show what you plan to write later and leave that answer for a while. You might just need a break, or you could decide to complete your next answer and then come back to the answer that was giving you trouble.
- You will still be nervous, perhaps more nervous than you had anticipated, so you can expect strange things to happen to your writing, as would happen in an on-campus exam. You might decide that you are writing nonsense, you might lose the thread of your thought, you might suddenly feel anxious, you might forget what you have just written. If this happens to you, take a short break and get some air or a drink or snack. You will not really have been writing rubbish, and being able to take a little break like this is one of the key benefits of an online exam.

ONLINE
HURDLE

Being alone for an exam can make you even more nervous than if you were in an exam room, even though there are many benefits. Some students we spoke to had made contact with their friends online during the exam time, hoping for reassurance and, perhaps, some guidance that they were on the right lines with their question choices and their answers. It seems to have been a disaster. They were demoralised by what they heard back from friends, who had taken a completely different approach. In one case the panic of an exam had led our student to misunderstand the helpful advice a friend gave her, with the result that she left out an entire question.

- When you have finished an answer (or the whole paper, if you prefer) checking is going to be as vital as it is with any exam. You have the benefit of enough time to check thoroughly, so make the most of it.

Once the exam is done, try to forget all about it. You might want to check briefly with a trusted friend to make sure that you did not make a major blunder but, beyond that, get on with your life – especially if that means getting on with preparing for the next exam.

How do I get higher marks?

Although any type of exam offers the potential for you to improve your exam technique, finesse your revision skills and develop your understanding, some aspects of online exams are especially useful in increasing your marks. Usefully, rather than waiting for time and more exam experience to help you, there are three things you can do before your next exam that can help you achieve higher marks.

Knowing in advance how you will tackle the exam

We have mentioned this several times in this chapter. Your confidence will be higher and your determination to succeed much stronger if you know what the path ahead of you will look like. Shaping that path yourself is the best way to guarantee that it is right for you.

Tailoring your exam to your knowledge

Taking control of the situation will always help you in an exam. That means being clear about what you know and how you can use your material. Mock exams

ONLINE
HURDLE

It is tempting to set up online groups with friends so that you can revise together and compare your revision notes. Although this is easy to do, be careful about whether it is really for you. Your revision notes might quite rightly be rather different from someone else's, because you are different people, with diverse ways of remembering and, perhaps, different ideas on how you want to approach the exam questions. Revision groups can also swallow up a lot of your time; if you have not chosen to be part of a revision group before, be cautious about it now.

Developing your material and technique

For exam success you need to get yourself in the right headspace for what you are about to do, regardless of whether the exam is online or in an exam hall. This means transforming your material from something that is static to a resource that is considerably more active, and you can do this by using your material. The most common, and usually the most effective, way to achieve this is to give yourself a mock exam, but with online exams you have new options.

Top tip

Even though any mock exam you give yourself as part of your revision schedule is going to be different for an online exam, it is still a clever idea to spend any mock exam time in the room in which you plan to sit the exam itself. Even for an online exam, practising in that room will help prepare you mentally for what is to come.

A mock exam is intended to replicate the exam situation as nearly as you can so that you get used to the feeling of an exam (so calming your nerves) and you can test out the material you have ready in your mind (so testing how well your revision is going). The beauty of an online exam is that the first of these is greatly reduced for you now. You will want to do some form of mock exam, but because you will probably be in familiar surroundings for the exam itself, and you might not be tied so tightly to time, you need not give yourself a trial of a strict two-hour exam so as to prepare yourself emotionally for the event.

This leaves you, potentially, with more revision time to spare for testing how well you know and can use your material, and this might persuade you to change how you do things for those exams where a short answer or an essay-type answer is required.

and practice tests will help you with this and an online exam could give you the time and online headspace to perfect your exam technique.

Using your time wisely

By thinking through the case studies in this chapter you will be able to decide how you want to use your time. This will have to be your choice, because you will be factoring in your private circumstances, the space and time available to you where you are working, and the type, frequency and number of exams you have to take during the exam period. Once you have decided on your best approach, try to stick to it in your first exam and then take a little while to reflect on it after the event. If it worked well, you have your best timing formula for your future online exams.

What do students think?

Student quotes

'Once I had a system in place and knew how to use my time well, I was able to perform better.'

'I was so nervous in my first online exam that it took me ages to settle my brain into what I was doing, but after that I was OK.'

'I much prefer online exams - being in my own space is way better than an exam hall! I am dreading going back to on-campus exams.'

All the students we spoke to seemed to agree that feeling confident in online exams has to do with becoming familiar with your own way of approaching the challenge and then having faith in how you do things. With the benefits of online exams, and despite some hurdles, we are not surprised to learn that many students now prefer them to on-campus exams.

Moving ahead

Moving on from an exam successfully comes in two parts: being ready to ignore it once it is over (there is nothing you can do now) and being ready to listen to feedback. Reading Chapter 10 on feedback is a good way to start well on that journey.

9

Online assessed tutor–student conversations and vivas

Discussion assessment, which can take the form of tutor–student conversations, including professional conversations, and vivas are well-established ways to engage with students and assess their knowledge and understanding in an 'in the moment' way. This does not mean, however, that students are put 'on the spot'; there is always time to prepare, and this chapter will show you how to do this effectively, so that you can face the online challenge with confidence.

What is an assessed viva or tutor–student conversation designed to show?

It is important to keep in mind that this form of assessment is designed to give you the chance to show off your knowledge and to gain good marks. Whilst assignments that are created and submitted by you ready for marking are fixed and cannot be changed during the marking process, a discussion assessment gives you the chance to respond to questions to show off your understanding in a way that is not always easy in fixed assignments. It also gives your assessors the chance to help you in this by leading the discussion for you.

What is involved?

Vivas

A viva (which comes from the Latin term *'viva voce'*– 'with the living voice') is a discussion designed to help an assessor confirm a student's ownership of a body of work, or evaluate core understanding of the topic and/or clarify any points that the work itself might not fully explain. This is a fantastic opportunity for students to show off their understanding of the topic in a much more fluid situation, responding to questions posed by the assessor, which might lead on to an aspect they had not fully explored in their work. A viva can help to add marks to a student's grade as the assessor can delve more deeply into the understanding and opinions of the student. This is particularly useful if you are a borderline grade student and might just tip you over into a higher level.

A viva requires an assessor to have prepared questions designed to check the student's competency and understanding within a topic. These questions should be fair and be based upon the student's submitted work, which may be a performance, art installation or written assignment. If the student has shown excellence in their work then the questions chosen will be designed to allow the student the opportunity to excel in their viva.

A viva will be arranged at an appropriate time after your work has been submitted to give you time to prepare. You should expect to answer questions based upon your submitted work. You may receive the initial questions the assessor is planning to ask, to help you prepare, but this is not necessarily the case in all situations, so make sure you check on this.

Tutor–student discussions

For some courses, you might find that you have assessed tutor–student discussions. These are less formal than vivas and professional discussions but are still equally valuable in their content and the impact that they can have on your final grade. A discussion like this will be arranged as a way for your tutor to ascertain your knowledge on a particular subject or module and therefore revision is certainly necessary. The tutor will have prepared questions to ask you to draw out information but will also go with the flow should the conversation veer off on a relevant tangent.

This more informal discussion style is ideal for enthusiastic explorations of texts and ideas, which can then be utilised in essays or future assignments. The tutor may be jotting down notes on the discussion as it proceeds or may even record it, so be prepared for this and do not let it fluster you. This is an ideal opportunity to raise your grades and can be an enjoyable and productive discussion as long as you prepare well.

Professional discussions

LECTURER'S
VIEWPOINT

Our students have told us how valuable they find professional discussions on their course, as this helps to prepare them for job interviews and the workplace.

A professional discussion usually occurs on vocational courses. For each module/course you will receive one or several assessments and each of these assessments will have a list of marking criteria. A professional discussion can be used as a way of increasing your marks or for covering criteria you have missed in your previous assessments.

A professional discussion will be based on prepared questions to ensure that you are able to cover missing criteria and is a formal discussion. You might have this assessment with your tutor, or it may be that an external professional is invited in for this assessment. Equally, it might be one-to-one or a group discussion with peers and professionals. Be sure to know who will be involved prior to the event so that you can prepare.

The professional discussion is likely to be recorded as it is a formal assessment and, much like an essay, can be assessed through formal assessment criteria. Check if there is to be a video or a voice recording as this may have some bearing on how the screen is laid out for you and how you wish to present yourself.

A professional discussion is often based on a dilemma scenario question that you may find in a work situation and asks you to discuss how you would resolve it. In this way you will be utilising what you have learnt on the module or course alongside your reasoning skills. This may be an individual or group task and so knowing which it is will be important in working out whether you are being assessed on working as a team and on people management skills as well as your knowledge and reasoning skills.

A viva, tutor–student discussion or professional discussion may occur mid-way through the academic year, as a way of assessing your progression through the course, or it may be an end-of-year assessment to complete the topic or module.

How is the online version different?

Unusually this form of assessment is almost unchanged by moving to an online format. There are benefits and limitations of holding discussions online, as we will discuss throughout this chapter, but there is no need to learn a lot of new technical skills, and there is less chance of things going wrong than there might be in other assessments.

Holding your assessment online might lead you to respond in one of two ways: either you will feel too relaxed as you are in familiar surroundings and will not take the time to mentally prepare yourself, or you might feel more anxious as you are unsure how an online discussion will work. Ideally, we want you to feel somewhere in between these two things: we want you to reach a point of confidence, and even excitement, at the prospect of discussing your topic. On that note, the secrets to feeling confident are knowledge and time. Know when your assessment is, how long it is expected to last, who will be present, whether it will be recorded and what the discussion will be based upon. Armed with that knowledge, take the time to explore the platform on which the discussion will be held as knowing the functionality will assist in the smooth running of the conversation. Also take the time to psych yourself up for the event. When you are physically going to an exam your brain naturally tunes into what is going to happen and you start running through scenarios in your head. With an online discussion, this is not necessarily the case, so make sure you take the time to mentally prepare yourself.

LECTURER'S VIEW

Some of our students have commented that they set themselves a routine to help get their brains into the right mindset for online assessment tasks. This may include setting up their workstation, getting a drink of water and sitting down in the same chair each time. This routine quickly engages their brain into exam conditions ready for what they are about to do.

At the start of the assessment, you can ask your assessor whether it would be acceptable to make notes in the chat function, or in a separate document, as the discussion progresses. Do not let this become a distraction, but it can be useful as a reminder if there are several parts of a question. So often, as someone asks you a question, you think of three things you want to say in response but, by the time you get around to talking about them, you have forgotten one of your points. Equally, the assessors might mention a relevant article or author that they suggest you read, and you can ask them to put this in the chat for you to research later. Remember, some platforms do not automatically save the chat so copy and paste into a Word document before the meeting is closed.

Establish the rules at the start of the online meeting. This is quite often done by the assessor but, if it is not, then feel confident about setting out how you would like to work. It might be that you want to write notes in the chat as a mini-agenda to follow as various points are raised in the discussion; you may have to ask for sharing rights from the host if you will want to share your screen during the meeting; you may want to confirm how you will take turns online in a group situation, such as raising your hand. Setting out these processes at the start of the meeting can reduce confusion later on.

One of the potentially lovely things about an assessment online is that you are not having to sit face-to-face with the assessor, worrying about making enough eye contact. Talking about your project or research to a screen can be easier, and more freeing, than being in the room with the assessor. You can choose how you want to view everyone and yourself. Being able to see yourself on the screen can help you recognise when you are coming across as anxious or defensive.

When someone is questioning your work, it can be an automatic response to feel defensive but, remember, the questioning is designed to help you elaborate on your wonderful piece of work. Everyone in the room wants you to get the grade you deserve. Seeing yourself onscreen can help you to relax. You can also see everyone else onscreen without them knowing which one person you are looking at. This means you can choose where you look much more freely and so, if there is a particularly stern-faced assessor, you can choose not to look in that direction when you reply.

You also have the benefit of seeing each person's background; seeing their homes or offices can give you more of a sense of the person as a human being rather than as simply an assessor. Recognising their individuality can help you connect with them more as people; for example, if you see they have similar books to you or artwork you like then you might feel more favourably towards them, helping you to relax into the conversation.

At the start of the conversation take the time to greet everyone and follow the social niceties of a traditional setting. This will help to set the tone and ensures that you know who everyone is, allowing you to use people's names when replying to questions. As you are working online it will not be obvious if you are talking to a specific person so make sure you use names when asking questions to clarify.

Top tip

Often you can hover your cursor over the person's image in a communication platform and it tells you their name and title. In other platforms it automatically has their name under their image.

Check prior to the meeting whether it will be recorded and shared and who will have access to this. If you want to review the recording when writing a reflective essay or if you want to go back and check a fact for a future research project you will need to know how to access the clip. It is also useful to know who will see this and how a professional conversation or tutor–student discussion will be graded. Is this being sent away to be externally assessed or will the person leading the discussion be marking it?

What do I need to know?

Much like a live conversation you will need to know the who, what, when, where, why and how of the meeting.

- Who will be present and what are their roles in the discussion; is it as the principal examiner, the second marker or the notetaker, for example?
- What is the conversation designed to draw out and which assessment criteria will be achieved through this discussion?
- When will the conversation take place and how long has been allocated to complete it?
- Where is the conversation taking place? In a live setting this will be a given room number whereas online you will be sent a link to an online platform. Make sure you take the time to familiarise yourself with this platform prior to your assessment.
- Why is this assessment taking place? Which criteria are you trying to achieve?
- How is the meeting meant to proceed? Is it a question and answer style format or a more general discussion?

Skills

One of the skills you will be able to showcase through any of these forms of assessment is your ability to talk with confidence and knowledge on your chosen subject.

ONLINE
BENEFIT

A discussion that takes place online is becoming increasingly familiar to us all, and you will have the benefit of being in a familiar space as it takes place, which can help you feel more comfortable and confident.

A viva might feel more like a presentation of your ideas as it tends to be less conversational than the other assessment methods. Each question will be open-ended meaning you will have the time to speak at length about your work. This is not a short question and answer session but a platform on which you can explore and explain your working methods, your research and your opinions.

Top tip

A vital skill in any discussion is being able to listen actively to the assessors as they will be asking you the questions and guiding you in your conversation.

There will not be any trick questions; the questions will be designed to guide you through the discussion with the aim of confirming your grade or assisting you in gaining more marks. Actively and accurately listening to, and answering, the questions will be key to gaining those extra marks. The assessor will be unbiased but will aim to guide you through the meeting with the questions they ask. If you stumble on an answer, they will ask a clarifying question. Knowing this can be reassuring in what could be a nerve-wracking situation. Listen to, and answer, each question concisely and coherently. If you need to ask the assessors to repeat the question or to elaborate, do not be afraid to do so. This is your assessment and you can control how it proceeds by asking for repetition or clarification, or by introducing and expanding upon ideas behind your submitted work.

Another useful skill to develop is knowing how to create a feedback loop. The assessor will ask you a question, you will answer it and then you will ask if that answers the question. In this way you are giving the assessor the opportunity to rephrase the question, ask additional questions and confirm that you have answered fully. This loop allows you to know that you have answered each question to the best of your ability, giving you confidence to move forward from your answers and on to the next question.

Each type of assessment will require you to develop and utilise skills which can be transferred into your working life. In the case of vivas and professional discussions, being able to hold a discussion in a professional manner, answering each question concisely and fully whilst responding to body language and facial expressions are all transferable skills. You can use your assessment as a way of practising your professional conversational skills, which will be useful for job interviews and in the workplace.

Top tip

Non-verbal communication (NVC) comprises up to 93% of all communication; NVC includes facial expression, body language and eye gaze. This means that only 7% of communication is verbal. Bearing that in mind, you should be aware of how you present yourself in your assessment.

As this is a formal assessment based upon how you communicate, and knowing that communication relies largely on visual aspects, consider what you are wearing, how you sit or stand, what you are doing with your arms and hands, and where you are looking when you are answering the questions. All of these visual clues will give the assessors clues as to how confident and comfortable you are in answering the questions. It can also warn them if you are prevaricating. If you appear relaxed, open and confident then the assessors will trust that you know what you are talking about and the communication between you will flow smoothly.

Although the viva is a chance for you to talk about your work, make sure that you leave space for the assessor to ask follow-up questions and try not to waffle. It is better to leave a pause to consider your answer before responding rather than rushing into an ill-considered response. This is particularly important if you are faced with a difficult question or a question with many parts. You can always ask the assessor to elaborate if you are unsure what the aim of the question is or if you forget part of the question during your reply. Remember to be polite and honest. This is not a job interview where you are trying to sell yourself. This assessment is meant to allow you to elaborate and show off your knowledge.

Top tip

If you do not know the answer to a question then try to find a neutral response, such as 'I had not thought of it from that perspective before', to show you are acknowledging the question. Take a moment to consider it. Take your time, but if nothing comes to you then be honest. If you suddenly think of an answer to a previous question, then find a suitable moment to revisit this question later on in the discussion or feed it into another answer.

A professional or tutor–student discussion will, like a viva, also entail answering questions but is much more about the flow of ideas and communication. The assessor will be speaking less than you as their role is to frame your responses with suitable questions and additions; the ideas and findings should come from you as the assessment is designed to assess your knowledge and skills and not those of the assessor.

This assessment style is purely based on the dialogue that happens at that specific time and place and, therefore, working out how to create smooth communication across an online platform is going to be paramount to the success of the assessment. We will discuss how to approach an online discussion later in this chapter, but it is worth mentioning here that being computer literate and being familiar with the various communication platforms will be a significant factor in this type of assessment.

Knowledge

The key thing here, as with most types of assessment, is having a robust and broad range of subject knowledge. With this, you will gain confidence in your ability to convey your knowledge and understanding in almost any assessment format. To streamline your revision process, make sure that you fully understand the marking criteria. Check any ambiguous points with your lecturer to ensure you are not revising something you do not need in the discussion.

You may receive the questions the assessor will be posing prior to the assessment, and this can help you to formulate and organise your ideas ahead of time. Sometimes you will receive this several days in advance, but it might be only half an hour before the assessment is to take place. If you only have half an hour to prepare, check whether you are allowed to use the internet or external resources to prepare or whether the discussion is restricted to your existing knowledge. A psychology exam, for example, might give you a choice of three dilemma-based topics and ask you to prepare one for a 10-minute conversation with your assessor. You would usually be allowed to use the internet to research and can take bullet-pointed notes into the assessment as long as this does not distract you from the conversation. This means you can jot down important names or dates, so you do not need to memorise them. If you have several days to prepare you can really delve into researching the topic and preparing potential answers.

ONLINE
HURDLE

It can be disconcerting when first making eye contact with people online as it might be they appear to be looking slightly off screen depending on where their camera is placed. Rest assured that they will be looking at you but they might also take the opportunity to look at their notes at the same time. These notes may be on their screen or to the side of their computer. In the same vein, you can also utilise this handy benefit of working online. Having your notes on the screen can make for a seemingly smooth delivery of an idea but be careful not to simply read your notes as then you risk becoming monotonous and losing the flow of the conversation.

Know who is in the room, whether and how it will be recorded and how long the assessment will be. As this is a discussion format you may be given flexibility on timing as there is an understanding that you might concisely answer each question, or you might want to elaborate on your answers. Be aware that, although you can prepare for the set questions, additional questions are likely to be added in response to your answers. These will be follow-up questions to clarify points or to assist you in finishing off a thought process.

ONLINE
BENEFIT

If you are face-to-face in a room, it can feel awkward to make a note of the questions as you are asked them, but to be able to jot down notes on your laptop as you talk can feel less intrusive and so less distracting.

Where do I go for help?

As this will be a small group meeting, whatever format it takes, then you can go directly to your tutor or assessor should you come across any technical difficulties or if you want clarification on what the purpose of the assessment is designed to show. They are likely to be able to sort out any problems quite quickly as it may be a case of sending you a new link or answering quick queries.

How should I prepare?

In vivas particularly, you will be asked questions relating to a particular piece of work. It might be that, in hindsight, you feel you could have improved or adapted your work in some way. Do mention this in your viva as this shows a good level of self-awareness and is a question that will almost certainly be asked. In a theatre degree, for example, you may be asked why you chose to perform in a certain style and why you did not choose to follow another artistic path. Being able to defend your choices and explain why you did not follow another route would, in this example, showcase your understanding of context, dramatic forms and alternative choices you could have made.

You are bound to be asked about anything that went wrong in your project or something that you missed, such as not including a leading critic in your research of a novel or not testing a scientific or mathematical hypothesis to its fullest extent. Although you have to be honest in answering this, you should use this assessment as an opportunity to showcase your skillset and knowledge.

Any assessed discussion is an opportunity to show your wider knowledge and experience and so you can talk around your topic in a way that would not be suited to an essay format. Bringing in real-life experiences, or a wider field of understanding, can show a connectivity of thought that enriches the discussion and shows off your understanding of the topic's place within a wider context. Having said this, try always to come back to the original topic and make sure that you are answering the question posed.

What is involved?

If you are undertaking a viva based on a group project, then it is imperative to be able to answer as a group. Check whether you are being marked as a group or as an individual. Check whether the marking criteria include teamwork; usually this is the case and so being able to answer as a team will be expected. Know why you, as a group, made certain decisions and created your final piece of work as you did. Take the time, throughout the creation process, to discuss alternatives and to question why you are making certain assumptions or decisions, as this will prepare you for your viva. It might be that you have taken notes throughout your working process, and these can be helpful in preparing for your discussion.

If you have been working as a group, then ensure that your notes match up and that you are on the same page prior to the assessment. It can be useful to have an online shared document that you can all view and develop so that you are literally all working off the same page. This document might also be sent to your assessor, and it could also help you to formulate a reflective piece of work after the assessed discussion.

If you are preparing material to use within your discussion then make sure you put it in an appropriate format: it needs to be easily accessible and coherent, on slides, in a Word document or as an image, for example. If the material is for your own use only, then bullet points will help you recall the essential information without disrupting the flow of conversation. If you wish to share the information in advance of the meeting, make sure you have it prepared and sent out a week in advance to give the other participants a chance to read it and create a response before your assessment.

It may be that you wish to share the document during the online conversation. On most platforms, you can share the screen to highlight which point you are covering; however, this may mean you and the other participants cannot see each other clearly on screen. This means you will lose the option to read body language and facial expression so will not necessarily know when someone wants to interrupt or how they are responding to the information. Some plat-forms will allow you to share your screen and the participants can resize the box showing you, to make you appear larger on their screen. Make sure you know which platform you will be using and then explore the functionality with a friend prior to the assessment.

You can prepare cue cards to rehearse with, if you wish, and this might be something you do with friends. Ask them to question you about the topic to give you a chance to practise several different responses. This can help you to reduce hesitations and the chance of mis-speaking. Try to move away from cue cards or reduce them down to bullet points before your assessment, otherwise they might hinder the flow of conversation and limit your ability to answer more fully.

You may want to prepare a couple of questions to ask the assessors during the assessment. This shows an awareness of the discussion format, and they might surprise you with their answers, leading you on to further discussion points. Make sure your questions are relevant and not too precise or too broad. If the assessment is testing your conversational skills, then being able to ask interest-ing and relevant questions will show your ability to develop a productive conversation.

Preparing visual material

If you are planning to share visual materials in your discussion, have them ready in advance and ensure that they can clearly be seen on the platform on which you will be working. Also make sure they are pertinent to the discussion. In a face-to-face meeting you have the luxury of having visuals as an incidental aspect to which you can casually refer. In an online assessment, they must become a crucial element, otherwise there is no point in taking the time to screenshare to show them. This is a positive aspect of having your assessment online, as you really have to think about the importance of the material you want to share, both visual material such as pictures, objects and videos, as well as what you want to verbalise.

Readying yourself for assessment

To prepare for any assessed discussion it is useful to work with a study buddy to ask you questions and to talk more generally about the topic. You will find that through this preparatory discussion you will recall material you want to discuss in your assessment and so it is certainly a worthwhile endeavour.

If you are not given access to the questions you will be asked in the assessment, then consider what might be asked and work on how you will answer. If some of your fellow students have been through this process it might be worth getting feedback from them about the format of the discussion and the style of questions that were asked. Be mindful, however, that this is not a guarantee that you will be asked similar questions, but you can be a bit more confident that the format of the discussion will be similar. This is particularly useful when working with an online discussion as the rules for how this will proceed can be different from a face-to-face discussion.

When working online you will not only have to consider how you are presenting yourself but also what your environment will be saying about you. Prepare your workspace to ensure that you have a well-lit space with a neutral background as this will be the least distracting and most professional choice. You will also need to dress fairly formally. Although it might be tempting to wear your pyjama bottoms and slippers, as they cannot be seen on the screen, this will not help you get into the right mindset for your assessment. Dress as though you were meeting face-to-face, although you might not want to wear an overly patterned or striped top as, onscreen, this can be highly distracting. Using a simulated background can cause you to blend in with it if you are wearing a similar colour, so check what you look like online prior to the assessment.

The benefit of working online is that you can hide any anxiety much more easily as nobody can see you wringing your hands under the table. The downside is that you may have to work that bit harder to manage the conversation as each of you may struggle to pick up on visual clues that allow a conversation to flow. However, this will mean that you have to be concise and coherent with your answers and potentially reduce the chance of you waffling.

> ONLINE
> HURDLE
>
> You are less likely to be able to pick up on body language and facial expression online and, therefore, you will have to work to ensure the communication is going smoothly. A way to overcome this hurdle is to make sure you are working on a big screen, so you have the best possible chance of viewing some of those visual clues. You can connect your computer to the television, for example, if this is a larger screen and so could help you. You can also 'pin' one or more people in the meeting to make their images larger.

When preparing for your discussion you will want to be careful in your language choices. Although the tutor–student discussion is slightly less formal than vivas or professional conversations, you will still want to use an appropriate range of language to showcase your vocabulary and your understanding of academic language and structures. You can prepare for this by reading scholarly articles, listening to academic debates and holding conversations with your peers based upon your assessment topic. You could also listen to BBC Radio Four as this level of language will help to hone your language skills.

When preparing for an assessed discussion, you may want to consider relaxation techniques to help reduce anxiety prior to, and during, your assessment. Some tips for prior to the discussion include preparing 'filler' statements to give yourself time to think, such as, 'You make an interesting point'. These give you a moment to think whilst acknowledging that the other person has said something. Before answering a question take a breath as, when we are nervous, we can sometimes take a shallow breath leading to running out of air halfway through making a point. Also, taking slow, deep breaths reduces heart rate and consequently lowers anxiety levels. During the assessment, or just prior, remember to relax your shoulders down and drop your tongue from the roof of your mouth. Both your tongue and your shoulders go up when you are feeling anxious and deliberately moving them down can reduce your sense of stress.

A wonderful benefit of working online is that you can move all your anxiety to below the computer screen, meaning you can be dancing a jig of nerves under the table and no-one will be any the wiser. Our suggestion is that, instead of a jig, you occasionally wiggle your toes. This can recall you to being 'in the moment' and stop you from worrying about the overall assessment; it can also make you smile and, when you smile, other people relax and smile back, creating a positive feedback loop.

What should I do on the day?

Set up your workspace and notes half an hour before the start of your assessment so that you are prepared and not rushing into the online room. Practise some relaxation and focusing exercises before the start of your assessment to get yourself in the right frame of mind. Dress appropriately and check the background. Also make sure that you will not be disturbed or have someone randomly walking behind you mid-assessment. With that in mind, also try to reduce any visual or auditory interruptions. If you are working in a busy environment, and you cannot find somewhere quiet to set up, then wear headphones as this will help to cancel out background noise for both you and your assessor.

When you are ready to enter the session, you can usually decide whether you want to enter the virtual room with your microphone and camera on or off. We would advise entering with both of these off. As it usually takes a few seconds to be fully 'in' the room, this will give you a breather and a chance to assess who is already in the room without being watched. It can also be disconcerting when everyone can see you before they have popped up on your screen so this will also negate that problem.

Try to enter the room a couple of minutes early and be prepared to make polite conversation. This time is so valuable for building a rapport with your assessors prior to the assessed conversation and can set you off on the right track for a smooth and enjoyable conversation. It also gives you a couple of minutes to fix any technical hitches and ask any clarifying questions before the assessment starts, such as 'Can you see and hear me okay?' or 'Would you mind if I make notes as we go along?' These are questions which usually come with the answer 'Yes', so you are setting up a positive element to your communication right from the start.

How do I get higher marks?

Much like an assessed presentation, an online conversation should not be rushed through and plenty of time should be taken to ensure clarity. If you talk at speed online you will find that points are missed and confusion can result. Remember that only a tiny percentage of communication is verbal. We all rely heavily on lip pattern, facial expression and body language. This takes a little more time and effort when conversing online so do not race through your information and keep checking back to make sure everyone is understanding it.

Look at the assessment criteria prior to preparing for your assessment and try to include the criteria wording in your responses. This shows that you have a clear understanding of the criteria and that you can answer each point of assessment. Preparation is important and making sure that your materials are relevant and accessible prior to the conversation will lead to a smooth assessment. If you want to share several visuals, then maybe consider grouping them so you do not have to flick back and forth between screen sharing.

Work with your tutor and/or your assessors to do well. This means asking for clarification prior to the assessment, and during the assessment, if it is needed. Do not bombard your tutor with questions that you can find the answers to elsewhere but do not be reticent about getting everything clear in your mind prior to the assessment. This communication should be an ongoing dialogue throughout the module or course they are teaching you, so you both have a better idea of each other's knowledge and communication style before you enter the assessment. It also means that the tutor will be able to recognise if you are nervous and come across as snappy in the assessment when you are normally friendly and effusive and can then try to remedy this and help you relax by asking you simple questions and trying to engage you in a non-challenging discussion prior to probing further into your work.

What do students think?

Students tend to find these sorts of exam to be very nerve-wracking as they are put on the spot, could be asked anything and are dealing directly with people who have more power than them in the situation.

Top tip

Taking control over what is within your power will reduce your anxiety. There is little point worrying over things you cannot change. Sometimes being able to control the smaller things, such as your work environment, how you enter the online space and how you present yourself, will help you feel more in control over the larger things.

Preparing for an assessed conversation can seem like a lot of hard work. We suggest you put it into perspective: how many marks is it worth? Knowing how this will affect your grade will help you decide how much preparation time to put into it.

Student quote

'It was less scary than I thought it would be because I knew my assessor from previous lectures, and they seemed genuinely interested in my work.'

Quite often, students are more open in online conversations as they are in a familiar environment and do not feel so intimidated by directly facing their assessor. Some assessments will be a tutor–student conversation with an external assessor observing. This is less noticeable online and the external assessor can even turn their microphone and camera off so as not to disturb the conversation.

Student quote

'I loved the chance to explain my work without a word count!'

Some students relished the chance to go beyond the limits of their other summative work. As there are no word counts, and the assessor's questions can help guide you, you can more readily demonstrate, not only your wider knowledge but also, your organisational, conversational and personal skills.

Moving ahead

An assessed conversation is rather like an interview and so can help you prepare for that challenge. You can ask for feedback to help you improve your conversational skills and this will be useful in future professional discussions. You can also use this feedback to help you when presenting or leading a seminar.

Top tip

Asking for tutor feedback about a completed assessment can feel redundant, but this feedback can serve as useful preparation for future assignments, so it is a worthwhile request.

Any discussions with your tutors will help you to build your relationship with them but an assessed discussion will be more formal and based on a specific topic. In this discussion you will be giving them an insight into your knowledge and opinions and therefore will, potentially, make a stronger bond with them. This insight will mean they are more likely to be able to guide you accurately along your learning journey.

Working with your tutor in a professional discussion will give you an insight into the professional world you are aiming to enter. You will be learning valuable skills such as presenting your ideas, taking on board other people's opinions and working with them, and managing a conversation.

Make the most of these types of assessment and ensure you reflect on the various topics and research avenues raised in the discussions. Communication is the key to unlocking ideas and moving forward in your research and life.

10

Making the most of feedback

It is easy to think of feedback as the end of a process: you have submitted some coursework or completed a task, you are given a mark and, alongside that hugely important mark, you are offered some feedback. When you think of the process in this way, it is clear to see why students can sometime see feedback as an afterthought. It is not unusual for a student to say to us 'I did not need to read your feedback – you gave me the mark that I was expecting.' If the mark is far lower than they expected, they sometimes avoid the hurt of reading comments, which, of course, is an understandable reaction.

The reality of feedback, however, is that it is not the end of the journey, but the start of a fruitful new journey, the beginning of a conversation that may last months or even years. Academics put huge amounts of effort into feedback in the hope that students will make the most of it and use that effort to propel themselves forward in their studies. In this chapter we will encourage you to see your feedback as a positive chance to improve your marks in future and we will show you ways to make the most of the opportunity online.

What is feedback designed to be?

- An overview – although your principal focus might naturally be on what the marker has said about the piece of work or an assessment activity that has just been marked, you will not want to miss the feedback that is more general. Every time markers write some feedback, or spend time giving face-to-face feedback, their aim is twofold: to help you understand why you received a particular mark, and to spur you on to do better in future. Differentiating between the immediate and the long term needs to be one of your goals as you receive feedback, in whatever form it takes.

ONLINE
BENEFIT

We will be discussing later in this chapter one of the great benefits of online feedback: your ability to save, edit and record feedback sessions or written feedback. This gives you far more time to seek out the immediate feedback and long-term pointers, rather than trying to do it in the moment.

- An active process – by taking the lead in some aspects of the feedback conversation (and this chapter will guide you in that) you can make sure that you glean every scrap of advantage you can from each piece of feedback you receive.
- A conversation – although you will be given feedback that your marker feels would be useful to you, that person cannot be in your head and so cannot know how well you are able to receive or understand the points being made. If you can be clear about what you have understood, what is not clear to you, and additional help and clarification you need, this will allow your markers to help you improve your marks.

LECTURER'S
VIEW

We know that sometimes students feel anxious about querying a comment in case it offends the marker or appears to be a quibble over the mark itself. You need not worry about this: markers will be confident in their judgement and so will assume that you are content with the mark too, even if it is not as high as you had hoped to achieve.

- A positive experience – but this is not entirely your responsibility, as your marker will be working to help you find the positive. You just need to be open to the chance to think about it positively, and sometimes this means taking your time and taking control of the situation where you can.

LECTURER'S
VIEW

We are sometimes surprised by what will upset a student whose work we have marked, but then we reflect that no student wants to be distressed by a comment, any more than we intended to cause upset. When a student asks us to explain in an email what we meant, or to delay a feedback meeting to give them more time to ponder what has been said, we are grateful that the student has been so open with us: it gives us the chance to make things right.

- A learning experience – it can be difficult to see feedback as a way to learn, until you flip your thinking to see it as part of a learning journey. Once you have done this, you are likely to face another hurdle: where is all this feedback that we are talking about? If you ask students what feedback they have received over a term they often talk only of a few pieces of feedback, usually written at the end of some coursework or in a formal feedback sheet online. There is so much more to it than that...

In the next section we will share with you what we recognise as feedback. Markers make space for feedback in many of your everyday learning activities, especially those online, and those students who recognise feedback when they see it are best placed to benefit from it and improve their overall performance.

What does feedback look like?

A student recently shared with us a feedback concern: 'I only received one very brief piece of feedback on the assignment, and I worked really hard on it. It seems unfair.' We soon realised that this was because he had only been explicitly told to look in one place for feedback, so he was understandably disappointed. Once we had identified with him the other three access points to relevant feedback he was much happier, but he is not alone in battling with this confusion.

This overview will help you identify the types of feedback you could actively seek out.

1. For written submissions you might see several sorts of feedback used together:
    o You might see detailed notes that have been made on your work throughout the assignment.
    o There might also be an overview piece of feedback, which makes more general comments on the piece of work.
    o If a marking rubric is being used, you could also see a set of marks or comments that go into the detail of your performance in a more structured, formulaic way.
    o You might be offered audio feedback, in the form of a short (2–3 minute) audio file.
2. For written exams you might not expect feedback but keep an eye on the situation. Sometimes feedback on the general exam performance is offered, or you may have the chance to receive specific feedback on your exam script, but this might be some time after the marks have been released, so this is something you might want to check with your lecturers or seminar leaders.
3. For practical lab work, assessed presentations and oral exams you might receive very little direct feedback during the event, as the focus will be on your performance, but you could look out for two types of feedback:
    o There might be an immediate feedback sheet that is either handwritten or typed during the event. This could be sent to you by email or scanned and uploaded to

your online marking area (you might expect this to be on your institution's Virtual Learning Environment (VLE)).

○ There might also be a more reflective piece of feedback, perhaps produced after the marker has seen several students perform and so is able to situate your performance within that wider frame of reference. This might be the feedback that focuses more on how you can move forward to your next challenge.

4. General module/course feedback is sometimes offered to students, but this is not always a requirement, and it can come out a little while after you have completed work on the module. It is easy to overlook this feedback or to do no more than skim-read it, but it is worth spending some time on it in case you can make links between what is said about this module and how it might relate to your next module.

5. Informal feedback is the most difficult to recognise, but it is sometimes the most useful and relevant feedback you can get, so we are sharing examples here to help you identify when this might be happening for you:

○ If you share a plan for an assignment with your seminar leader or lecturer, the discussion will mainly cover that particular plan, but it is bound also to include a wider discussion about your understanding of the material and your ability to form a persuasive argument or explain processes and theories clearly.

Top tip

After you have had a meeting to talk through your plan for an assignment, take time as soon as you can to spend 10 minutes reflecting on what has just happened. Was anything said that you can take forward as advice for future assignments?

○ Sharing ideas for a project can happen in passing, almost without you noticing it. You might be in a seminar or study group and the project (whether it is an essay or a more practical project) comes up in discussion. This is often when the best ideas bubble to the surface, so make sure you capture them in that moment.

LECTURER'S VIEW

Although this chapter has 'feedback' in its title, as educators we are used to thinking about 'feeding forward' as much as feeding back. Whilst we want to help our students to understand how we arrived at a mark for them, we are equally interested in helping them get better marks in future, and so feeding forward is always firmly in our minds. When it is also in the mind of a student, we know that we can make a real difference at every opportunity.

o   In a seminar you might be informally trying out some new ideas, theories or material that you are thinking of working up to form part of an assignment. If you do this as a deliberate part of your learning strategy, you will learn to hear, note and use the feedback that you are given in that informal setting.

ONLINE
BENEFIT

In an informal setting such as a seminar or study group, feedback on your ideas that you receive from other students can make a positive impact upon your learning journey, and online events such as these give you the chance to listen to suggestions and also see them in the chat function, which you can copy and paste so that you can consider them after the event. If you are unsure, taking the time to cut and paste and check in this way will allow you to approach your seminar or study group leaders to ask what they think about what has been suggested.

o   Meetings with your academic tutor can be wide ranging, and often they deal with general areas of your studying life in an informal way, but your tutor is also there to help you understand your feedback. If you do not understand what is being said in a comment, for example, or you keep seeing a comment that does not really make sense to you, an informal chat with your academic tutor will save you time.

Whether feedback is formal or informal, written or spoken, it is a huge time saver, and that is one of the primary reasons for engaging with it. There is no point in spending time and effort trying to take on a new and daunting challenge if the feedback (and feed forward) you have already received would make it easier for you. One of the best results of working with feedback is that you recognise your achievements and can reuse the talents that got you there.

How is the online version different?

In essence, online feedback is different in three important ways. It can allow you easier access to the person who marked your work, it gives you the advantage of being able to share documents and make notes or record conversations easily, and, for some students, discussing challenging feedback online and at a distance can feel more comfortable.

In practical terms, the places where you find feedback may have altered, and this can make the experience feel different. You will want to make the most of this chance to learn, so we are offering you an overview of how things might have changed with online learning and how you can make it work for you (see Table 10.1).

Table 10.1   Ways to make online feedback work for you

Feedback opportunity that is not online	Online option for that type of feedback	Top tips for making the online version work well for you
Detailed written feedback on work that you have submitted, which might have been inserted throughout the piece of work.	This might now be in a text box online and/or in comments that are on your assignment online.	1. Make sure you know the functionality of this feedback. If you see a single-word comment in a box on your online essay, clicking on it may open a far fuller comment. 2. If a marking rubric is used, the feedback you receive might be automatically generated from the mark that is awarded, so read it with this in mind.
Overview feedback on a written assignment, which might have been placed at the end of a piece of work.	This could be typed into a text box, or attached to a grading area, or sent to you as an MP3 or MP4 file.	1. Find out in advance if you should be expecting this type of feedback. It is less common and so it is easy to assume it is not there. 2. Consider using speech-to-text software to convert the audio file into a text file if you find written comments easier to digest or if you expect to refer back to a few specific details in future.
Feedback on exams that you have undertaken, which might have been given to a whole group in class.	This might now be written down and lodged on your institution's VLE.	1. Be patient and vigilant – this feedback might not arrive until some weeks after you sat the exam, but it will still be useful for your development. 2. Be ready to engage with feedback that relates to questions you did not answer in the exam – it can feel tedious to wade through the material, but you could find some nuggets of advice in there that suit you perfectly.

Feedback opportunity that is not online	Online option for that type of feedback	Top tips for making the online version work well for you
Feedback on events, such as presentations, oral exams or lab sessions that would have been written up at the time and given out to the participants, or written up after the event and circulated.	The immediate feedback, made perhaps on feedback sheets as you carry out a task, might be lodged online rather than given out. The more reflective feedback that you might use to feed forward is likely to be circulated as usual.	1. If the event is online it can feel deflating to put in the effort and leave the event without any sort of immediate feedback. Finding out in advance when you can expect some feedback will help you prepare for this. 2. Being offered feedback need not mean a mark is shared, so again check on this in advance. Will you be expecting a mark and feedback shortly after the event, or just feedback with a mark to follow at a later point?
General feedback on the performance of all students on a module for a particular assignment, which might have been offered in a face-to-face classroom situation.	This does still happen, but awareness of how tiring students can find learning time onscreen has led many markers and institutions to make this more formal. Markers are often asked nowadays to put this feedback in written form to be lodged within the VLE and sometimes also sent to students.	1. You might find some useful tips for other modules by looking at this type of feedback, so copying it and attaching it to your other feedback comments for a module can be a good way to make sure that you do not overlook it in future. 2. This feedback can be valuable to you as you approach your next modules (or even as you choose modules) because it shows what skills students needed in order to do well. It is somewhere you might consider looking when you are making module choices, as this feedback is often stored online for several years.

(Continued)

Table 10.1   (Continued)

Feedback opportunity that is not online	Online option for that type of feedback	Top tips for making the online version work well for you
Informal feedback, which might have happened at the end of a face-to-face seminar, or in a passing chat in the corridor, or in meetings when something else was the main topic of conversation.	This might come in the form of short sessions online with a lecturer or seminar leader, or during online learning events such as seminars or workshops, or in meetings with your academic tutor.	1. This type of feedback has always been tricky to spot and capture, by its very nature. It is easy to have a conversation and then forget exactly what you were advised to do in your essay because it was just a passing comment. Online makes this easier because you can keep a document open (or use the 'sticky notes' function on your device) ready to make notes as soon as the advice is given, even if you are in the middle of a seminar. 2. If a comment is made in the chat area of an online event, make sure that you capture it in the moment so that you can keep track of all this feedback and advice that is flowing your way.

Top tip

> We have recommended throughout this book the use of 'sticky notes'. These are little jotting areas that appear on your screen, looking like Post-it notes. They are a great way to capture your thoughts as you work with others online and they are available (under various names) on many devices.

We can trace here how feedback has moved now that more of it is online, and we see that as an advantage in many ways, but what is undeniable is that the 'feel' of feedback has also changed to some extent. For some students this change is minimal: within moments of being in an online feedback situation they feel at home and forget that they are not face-to-face. For others, the advantages of being online outweigh the challenge and they are happy. For some students, however, online feedback is difficult. They can struggle to make themselves clear online, or feel isolated and out of touch when they receive more challenging feedback.

If you find online feedback comfortable, the next few sections of this chapter will help you maximise the benefit to you; if you find online feedback challenging, you can use these sections to help you overcome most of the difficulties you face. This in turn will help you to develop a more positive view of feedback, which will make online feedback far more productive for you going forward.

> **ONLINE HURDLE**
>
> Chat areas of online meetings and learning sessions can disappear after the event, which can be very disconcerting, and could be disastrous if you were hoping to return to the chat to retrieve some vital information. Keep this in mind as you go: if you are working in an online area that is time-limited and will not make the chat notes available afterwards, copy and paste whilst you can.

The types of feedback we have included in Table 10.1 have one thing in common: they are all *offered to you* in one form or another. Your role is to recognise, capture, understand and act upon that feedback. However, if you are to take an active role in your learning through feedback, so that you can increase your marks in future, it helps to know where to go online to seek out feedback. Not every student will do this, and it will put you ahead of the game in your studying if you do.

In Table 10.2 we show you where to look for this type of feedback – and how it might help you.

Table 10.2 How to be proactive with feedback

Proactive feedback option	How you could use it
Student module evaluations	This is not the most obvious route to feedback, but it can be revealing. A module convenor's response to student feedback from previous years can sometimes give an insight into the ways a module – and its assignments – have been changed in response to student concerns. This is a nice example of their feedback feeding forward into your planning for assessment on the module.

(Continued)

Table 10.2 (Continued)

Proactive feedback option	How you could use it
Study groups	If you are in a study group with students who are taking the same module as you, but who are in different seminar groups, sharing general feedback (or advice) on an assignment that was offered in those different seminars can be a good way to deepen your understanding of what is expected in the next assignment. This could lead to rumours and conjecture, but as long as you are careful to check for accuracy, this can be a valuable feedback route.
Study advisors	There is a misconception amongst some students that study advisors are only there for those students who are struggling. This is not the case. Study advisors are there to help students excel, regardless of their current level of achievement. If you have a thorny issue that has been raised in feedback, find out about online study advice sessions that are open to you. It might only take one meeting to resolve a problem that might otherwise follow you for months.
Online support courses	We mean here any study courses or brief screencasts that are provided by your department or your university. It is becoming commonplace now for academics to offer such online support, which is leading to some very useful, short screencasts on aspects of assignments that students find tricky. These are often made in direct response to feedback that an academic is giving on a module, and will sometimes be lodged on your VLE, but might also appear on YouTube and similar. One note of caution: never trust a site you do not know (at least by reputation) and you should never need to pay for this type of advice and feedback.
Student support	You do not need to be expert in finding feedback: you just need to contact someone who is. Student support administrators/coordinators/advisors are there to make sure that, if you do not understand your feedback, or you need help making sense of a pattern of feedback, or you cannot find your feedback, you can go to exactly the right person to help you.
Librarians	Librarians deal with so much more than books. They can help if your feedback mentions the research and resources you have used in an assignment, and they can feed forward to how you might structure your approach to resources in the next assignment. They are usually available for one-to-one online sessions and offer a wide variety of online courses, instructions and group information sessions.

Proactive feedback option	How you could use it
Module convenor	You might not see your module or course convenors at all during the term, because they will have organised the courses or modules, but will not necessarily teach all (or any) of the seminar or workshop groups. This is unlikely to be the first person you approach for help with feedback, but is a useful person to contact if you need some module-level clarification on a point made in your feedback, such as the number of sources you used or the way in which you structured a report. This might also be a good person to know for future reference, when you come to make your next module choices.
Built-in help as you type	As we are writing this book, using Word online, little dialogue boxes keep popping up to tell us how many words we have mistyped, how many grammar errors the system thinks we have made and how we might improve the flow of our writing. We will ignore some of this advice – and you should too – but we are always pleased to receive this automated feedback as we go. Turning on all the help functions that are on offer to you as you produce an assignment (and these will not all be automatically activated) can give you instant feedback even before it reaches the marker, so, even if it irritates you a little, we urge you to try it out.

What challenges might online feedback bring?

Some of the challenges to successful online feedback are universal, regardless of how you are engaging with the person who is offering the feedback, so you need to prepare just as well as always. Take time to reflect on the feedback (and this might be a little while after your initial skim-read through, if you found any of the comments difficult) and make a note of all the questions you want to ask. List these in order of importance to you, in case you start to run out of time.

If you cannot think of any questions, this need not concern you. There are times when the feedback is so thorough and clear that you cannot think what to ask, but this is just telling you that the session could be brief. If you have looked at the feedback and your mark a couple of times and you cannot think of any questions, you might want to use the opportunity to ask the most pressing question: how do I get a better mark in future?

LECTURER'S
VIEW

We are often struck by how few students ask this obvious question about improving their grades. It might be shyness or modesty, but we spend time trying to feed forward in our comments and we enjoy being asked such a key question. In some circumstances, it can be the most difficult question for a marker to answer, but the answer will be both revealing and valuable to you.

Once you have your list of questions, be ready to type as you talk so that you can make a note of the feedback you are being offered. This is one of the significant advantages of online feedback sessions: rather than madly trying to make notes on a notepad on your knee during a meeting, you can make notes more easily and create them in a form that allows you to amend, enrich and copy them in future. This helps you to make the most of your feedback.

LECTURER'S
VIEW

When we are offering feedback to a student, we can easily forget that the student is trying to make notes as we go as it is not always obvious on screen. Your lecturer will be grateful to you if you ask for a pause as you make notes, so do not worry about doing this.

Knowing how to share your screen online is going to be important if you would like to show the marker your questions, or share the plan you have made for your next assignment based on the feedback you have just received. If you would like the marker to work on the document with you, you will need to know how to share the document on screen so that you can both write on it rather than the marker just looking at it.

Top tip

If you have any doubts about the length or format of a feedback session, or you are not sure who will be there, or you feel anxious about how you might feel, it is a good idea to make an edited, brief list of just the few most pressing questions you want to ask. You can share this list on screen, and then if you find that you have plenty of time and you feel at ease, you can share your original, longer list of queries and concerns.

Sharing a document on screen is one thing; showing your face has quite another feel to it. You can feel exposed and awkward if the marker sees your face as you discuss the feedback you have been given, and this is obviously not a comfortable position for you. This is an issue that is worth pondering for a moment. What makes you nervous is the human interaction that also makes for a good feedback session, with two people engaged in a conversation whilst they look at each other. On that basis, it makes sense to turn on your camera and take an active and positive approach to the learning opportunity.

But what about those awkward questions on your feedback that you used to be able to ask 'accidentally on purpose' when you met a marker in the corridor, or just at the end of a seminar as everyone was leaving? We are used to these questions, when students reveal that they are not sure about an aspect of writing, or they think they missed an instruction, or they might need more time in an exam. If your teaching, as well as your assessment, is carried out online, you can feel a bit lost. If this is the case for you, make the most of the chat function.

Lecturers are used to leaving space in their calendars, often straight after seminars, lectures or workshops, for just this type of query. A note in the chat asking the lecturer to linger online at the end of the session will give you the chance to raise an awkward query on your feedback. If several of your fellow students also have the same question, one of you could ask the question in the chat during the session and then sit back and wait for it to be answered. The seeming distance of online learning can sometimes be an advantage in this sort of situation.

At the end of every feedback session, you should be left with some questions answered, some suggestions for moving forward and, perhaps, some instructions about what to do next (perhaps, for example, some suggested reading or research). Hopefully, your needs will have been met and you can work through the notes you have made. However, what if this is not the case? You might be left with a vague impression of something important being said that you cannot quite recall in all its detail, or a reference being offered but you did not quite catch the name of an author.

We have urged you in this chapter to take an active approach to feedback, and this is a situation where you are positively advantaged by an online feedback situation. Just as you made a list of questions to ask before you arrived at the session, and made notes during the session, you can now peruse those notes and make more if you need to extend or edit the records you made. This is the time to give feedback on your feedback.

A brief email to the marker with these finalised notes attached is a good way to make sure that you have everything right. If you ask the marker just to take a look through and check that you have got everything down correctly and remembered all that was said, you might be pleasantly surprised to find that your marker adds a few more feed forward suggestions. In addition, that academic now remembers you as a student who is committed to using feedback productively, a student who is striving to do well.

ONLINE BENEFIT

Being able to record a feedback session has advantages, but this is not always possible, given the privacy protection that needs to be in place for both marker and students. This can be a good thing: some students spend hours poring over every detail of a recorded session rather than relying on the brief notes they made, and this works against them. Markers might also feel restrained by the fact that every casual comment is being recorded. If, having thought it through, you still want to record, then ask permission in advance of setting it up.

Are there benefits to me with the online version of feedback?

The main benefit of online feedback is that you can take so much more control of the situation. You do not need to wait to bump into an academic to ask a question: you can simply ask them to meet you online, or to stay behind in the virtual room after a learning session. You do not even have to ask a question aloud if you feel awkward or are concerned to be clear about what you need: you can use the chat area of a meeting or craft the perfect email to move things along. Feedback online often minimises the need to return to old ground or to repeat advice.

LECTURER'S VIEW

We encourage our students to type up their list of questions for a feedback session and then copy and paste the text into the chat area of our online meeting room. It can be a bit daunting if you are both faced with a huge list of queries to cover in a relatively short space of time, but it does act as a useful way to gauge how much ground needs to be covered. It can also save time and can help anxious students as they do not need to try to get a complicated feedback question across in the meeting – they have prepared exactly the right question in advance.

Another benefit of online feedback is the way in which you can take control of the feedback material. If you are using the chat area for making notes during a feedback session, you can cut and paste this into a document. If you are making notes as you go along in the meeting, you can send them to the marker for confirmation that you have recorded everything correctly; you can then cut and paste these notes into several places if you like. If you record the online meeting, you have back-up for future reference – although we would urge you to make sure that you take only brief notes from the recording. It can weigh you down to know that you have hours of feedback recorded and lurking on your computer, waiting for you to work through it.

Top tip

> If you are using an online setup that allows speech-to-text transcriptions, using it during feedback sessions can be a handy way to save you some note-taking time.

As you have control over the notes and automated transcript of feedback sessions, you might want to think about how to manage them. You could be using standard files and folders on your computer, or you could use an organisation system such as OneNote, but the principles remain the same. You do not want to be overwhelmed with feedback notes that start to feel like an inaccessible mountain of advice, so you could consider splitting these notes so as to make them more effective. If you were to do this, you could end up with:

- One complete set of notes from a feedback session, including the questions you planned to ask, the answers you received and the additional advice you were given. This can be filed in a folder called 'feedback' on your computer.
- This feedback folder will also include feedback you have been given on your work or your plans that was offered outside a feedback session (this would include all of the types of feedback, formal and informal, that we have mentioned throughout this chapter).
- As well as one folder that collates all of the feedback you receive, you could add a version of this complete set of notes to the folder you have on your computer for module documents for that particular module. This version is likely to be briefer and more to the point – very practical, immediate pieces of advice for your next assignment on the module (the feed forward parts of the larger document).
- You might also copy this briefer document into the folder for any module you are due to take later in your course, if the relationship between the two modules (and their assessment) is close enough to make this worthwhile.
- Each time you make notes on feedback, from any source, think about patterns of feedback. Patterns are likely to emerge that are relevant to everyone (they keep telling us to end our presentations with a certain type of slide) or that particularly relate to your

work (markers keep telling me that I am losing marks because I cannot work out how to use paragraphs effectively). Keep a note of these snippets of feedback in a document called 'feedback patterns'.

- In your feedback pattens document, you might divide the material into three: the advice that is relevant to the very next set of assignments that are due (remember to double space and include the title of the project before I submit), the guidance that will help you as you move on to your next modules or course (make sure that I plan more thoroughly on fieldwork projects) and the information that does not make sense to you yet (what is a comma splice, and why should I care?).

Does this sound like hard work, and time consuming? We agree, it is, but that is good. Reflecting on feedback, converting it to feed forward and applying it to your next assignment can be very difficult to do. You are having to undo patterns of thinking and writing or change the way you approach an entire topic area, or reassess how you present your ideas, and none of that is easy. By working through your feedback and feed forward notes like this you are making that process far easier. Each time you interrogate your notes to decide how to divide them, or reduce them, or file them, you will be reflecting on the content. You might never need to look at some areas of the notes again, because you learned the next lesson you need almost without realising it. So, if you find that you have done all this work and then you hardly refer back to one set of notes, you need not worry: they have just done their job for you.

What do I need to know?

In this section we want to touch on the relationship between your marks and your feedback, so that you know where you stand if you receive a mark that is lower – or higher – than you were expecting.

If the piece of work that is being marked counts towards your overall module or course mark (called a summative assignment), then the batch of submissions should be second marked in some way. This might take the form of every piece of work being marked by two (or more) people collaboratively, or each assignment being marked by one marker and then double-checked by another marker. It could take the form of moderation, where a sample of pieces in a batch is checked by a second marker. External examiners (academics from another department or university) will also be involved in the assessment process.

What this knowledge gives you is reassurance that marks for the work you submit are not awarded lightly or without careful thought based on much experience, and this is the reason it is highly unlikely that you will be able to appeal against a mark on the basis that you are unhappy with it or disagree with the assessment of your work.

You might already be aware of this rigorous marking process, but what is sometimes less obvious to students is that the feedback, too, is scrutinised in this process. This is important for you in your learning journey, because it means that you can rely on the feedback you are offered and you will know that the feedback, in the view of academics, relates well to the mark you were awarded.

So, if you receive a high mark, yet your feedback is peppered with feed forward comments, it is because the marker believes that you could achieve even higher results in future. If you receive a lower mark than you had hoped and yet the comments seem surprisingly upbeat, it is because the marker has pointed out the few things that reduced your mark significantly and then wants to focus on what you did well, because that is what the marker wants you to build on in future.

Top tip

Although we want to reassure you that the marking and feedback process is scrutinised and thorough, any system can have glitches. If you receive a very low mark and yet the feedback is effusive and full of high praise, it is still a good idea to check that your mark is what was intended, rather than an error.

Where do I go for help?

Although we have signposted you throughout this chapter to different sources of support, you might find it useful to have this guidance in one place (Table 10.3).

Table 10.3   Sources of help

What do you need?	Where could you go?
When are the marks released for me to see them?	This information should be online, either in the form of a set date for each assignment or in a university policy about a standard number of working days before marks are released. If you cannot find it, your student support coordinators/advisors or course administrators will know.
Where do I find my online feedback?	Even on a single module or course, there might three or more places you would need to go online to find feedback, depending on the assignment type. If you cannot find it, and there do not seem to be any instructions to help you, ask your seminar leader; you will not want to be hunting for it at the moment you receive your mark.

(Continued)

Table 10.3   (Continued)

What do you need?	Where could you go?
How do I contact the marker for some feedback?	It helps to know this in advance of the marks being released. Assignments are often marked anonymously, so markers do not know they have marked your piece of work. If you know who marked the work, ask in advance how they like to be approached – they might be happy to receive an email or they may have set aside time slots for feedback on an online appointment system. If you do not know who marked the work, contact the module/course convenor.
What if I am still struggling to understand my feedback on an assignment?	If you feel unclear about an aspect of your feedback even though you have had a feedback session, go to your academic tutor for help.
What if I keep being given the same piece of feedback?	This type of feedback pattern is useful to you as it means that you can go to a study advisor with a very specific query, which can often be the start of a productive and more wide-ranging conversation.
Who can help me understand how the feedback is structured?	At the start of a module, it makes sense to ask about how feedback and the marks are structured. Is there a marking rubric so that a set percentage of marks are available for a particular aspect of the work? Is the feedback generated from that rubric? Or will the marker be marking more freely, with marks awarded on the overall quality of the work? By knowing the marking structure in advance, you can prepare your assignment accordingly and understand how your feedback is produced.
I think I must have missed some key points in my module – who can help?	Approach the module or course convenor/organiser.
I feel demoralised by my feedback but where should I turn for help?	Your fellow students will help, especially if you are in a regular study or revision group. It may be that they are receiving similar feedback and so can help you understand it better, which can often help. If you still feel demoralised, consider explaining the problem to your family or go to the wellbeing or counselling service within your university. You deserve this support and it is there for you, so make the most of it.
I want higher marks – who can help me with ideas and guidance on how to improve more generally in my work?	Your academic tutor can help with this, but so too can any study or peer-assisted learning group in which you are involved. Getting higher marks is an important part of your study journey, so take the time to consider which aspect of your feed forward you want to share with others at each stage of your learning.
I am finding the idea of feed forward challenging – is this just me?	No! It is the most challenging aspect of feedback. Ask your academic tutor or a study advisor to help you break it down into manageable chunks so that you can take a step-by-step approach to improvement.

How should I prepare?

Preparing well for a feedback session guarantees that you can make the most of it. Here is a checklist to help you:

1. Are you sure you know which assignment is being discussed, if you have submitted several? Or is this a more general feedback session?
2. Are you ready to make notes?
3. Will you be alone with the marker online or is this a group feedback session?
4. Do you have a copy of the relevant assignments to hand so that you are ready to talk in detail?
5. Have you checked how the mark you have been given fits into your typical marks? Having done this, should you be especially proud of a high mark and so looking to feed forward to even higher marks in the future, or was your mark low enough to make you concerned?
6. Do you understand any written comments you were offered, and have you made a note of any that you did not understand?
7. Can you see a trend in your feedback across several assignments that might lead you to ask about one specific comment in this piece of feedback?

What do I do on the day?

We have discussed feedback sessions in this chapter as if they are the easiest event you could attend, and often they are. If you are simply given some group feedback on an assignment in a lecture or seminar, you can almost overlook the fact that you are being offered feedback. Your challenge in many instances is to spot when feedback or feed forward is being offered so that you can benefit from it. However, if you attend a session with a marker that has been deliberately set aside for feedback, you can feel unexpectedly nervous, and this is under-standable. This person is about to talk through your work in detail; what was a private activity, a piece of work produced in your own space and time, is now shared and so you feel more exposed.

Here are some guidelines to help you:

*   Always be ready – if you have not had time to prepare your questions before the meet-ing, ask for it to be postponed.
*   Make sure the marker is ready – email some or all questions in advance if you think that would help you both, or copy and paste them into the chat area when you get into the meeting.
*   Know how much time you have – a meeting set aside for half an hour is likely to be followed directly by a feedback meeting with another student. If you need longer, ask for a double slot so neither you nor the academic giving you feedback are being rushed.

- Take a friend – if you know that you will be very anxious, think about asking if you could have a joint feedback meeting with a friend on the course who has completed the same assignment – this could help you both.

ONLINE BENEFIT

For online feedback sessions it is easy to ask a friend to sit in the background and take notes for you, so that you and the marker can focus exclusively on having a productive conversation. Tell your markers that you are doing this so that they are not concerned about the fact that you do not seem to be taking notes, or startled by hearing someone else in the session.

How do I get higher marks?

There is a final but important point we need to share with you as this chapter concludes. Feedback is based on human interaction and an open conversation, where the marker knows where you are coming from, and this is the best guarantee that it will work well for you both. So, it is fine to say how you feel during a feedback session. Indeed, it can be very useful. If you begin by saying that you are nervous about receiving feedback, but that you are keen to progress and so want to make the most of the opportunity, the marker will know how to support you best and will recognise your commitment.

What do students think?

Student quote

'It took me a while to turn my brain around to realising that feeding back is really about feeding forward.'

We liked the way our student put this, and it is a common response to getting your head around feedback. It is hard work trying to use what you are learning about your past work by putting it into improvements in your next piece of work, but it is never wasted effort.

Moving ahead

If, at the end of feedback sessions, you show that you have listened carefully and you thank the markers for their time, you are building a good feed forward relationship. If you then follow up by sharing some notes (if this would help you) so that your markers can confirm the advice that was offered, you are set more steadily on your journey. If you then keep your feedback conversation going, by talking over aspects of feedback with other supporters, you are moving firmly towards higher marks.

After all of that, if you collate and manage your feedback notes so that you can make best use of them as you approach the next challenges, you can ensure that even a brief piece of advice is utilised to improve your marks. We were once told by a wise student that feedback is a gift, and should be received in that spirit. This chapter will have helped you to ensure that it is a gift that will keep on giving for the rest of your study journey. We hope that this book will also be a gift that keeps on giving. Good luck!

Helpful terms

Academic integrity   This is about honesty in your academic studies, including correctly acknowledging and referencing other sources.

Academic misconduct   This includes all actions that are devious in the attempt to achieve an academic qualification. For example, plagiarism, cheating, taking materials into an exam that are not permitted, completing someone else's work, and so on. Your university will have guidance on how to avoid this.

Analyse   This question type does not demand a description and if you feel that you must describe something first, keep it to one or two sentences as it is unlikely that you will get any marks for this. To analyse something is to methodically examine it in order to explain and interpret what has gone on and why.

Assessment   This is a method of collecting information from you to check your level of knowledge/skill/understanding.

Assessment criteria   These are a set of predetermined conditions that a piece of work will be assessed against. They are designed to test every candidate fairly and to enable the assessors to standardise their marking.

Assessment Delivery System (ADS)   The software, hardware and telecommunications systems, along with the humans involved, in delivering an assessment.

Attachment (file attach assessment type)   This is a computer document or file that you can 'attach' in an online system to submit work. Your institution is likely to use an assessment submission platform for your assessments rather than the more old-fashioned system of handing in paper copies of your work.

Audio capture assessment type/Audio file   This is a sound recording that you would make for your assessment. This will need to be clear and be compatible with your institution's systems to be marked.

Compare   Comparative essays will be based on two or more subjects. It is important to balance your argument and identify the similarities and differences between the things that you are comparing.

Competency-based assessment   This is usually a pass/fail type of test and is a term most often used with practical subjects such as mechanics, medicine and so on.

Computer adaptive test   In these tests the assessment programme will reveal the next question as you go along, responding to the input of your previous answer(s). The drawback of this type of test is that you cannot go back and edit your responses.

Delivery method   This is how you will receive your assessment: online, offline, on-campus, remotely or paper-based.

Describe   A question asking you to 'describe' something requires you to give a detailed account. Try to avoid speculation and instead stick to the facts of the subject.

Diagnostic test   This test is used to determine which level of a course you are working at. For example, if you have some competency in French but you have never undertaken an assessment for it then you would be issued a diagnostic test to establish which class to join.

Digital logbook   This is mainly used for practical skills and supports the summative assessment. For example, in a qualification that requires a certain amount of hours in the workplace (such as for counselling qualifications), you would record it in this way.

Download   To make a local copy of a document (usually from an online source) on your device or onto your Cloud.

Drag-and-drop type question   These are like multiple-choice questions in some ways but the answers are listed and you use the computer mouse to drag and drop the correct answers into place.

E-assessment   An assessment that is carried out (at least in part) through the use of technology.

Either/or question type   As you might be able to guess from the title, these questions require you to respond to closed questions such as yes/no questions.

E-learning   This differs from the old-fashioned term 'computer-based learning' as it includes learning involving the internet and internal networks.

Electronic marking and feedback   As you will submit your work online, you will also receive your marks and feedback online. This may come in the form of audio feedback in short audio files, or written commentary.

End point assessment   Usually found used in the more vocational subjects or a subject with vocational ties, this is used to assess your progress and final competency.

Essay-style question type   A question that requires a long answer using full sentences and a breadth and depth to the ideas and thoughts you are sharing.

Evaluate   An evaluation is to assess the worth or value of something. For example, if you are asked to evaluate a play scene, you should be looking at what happened and how that has contributed to the overall play.

Exams officer   The academic in the department who is responsible for ensuring that the exams are running smoothly. You would approach them if you are having trouble with accessing or completing your assessment for a practical or technical reason.

Explain   In a question beginning with 'explain', you should make the idea(s) clear to your audience. It is not purely a description but goes further and is often followed with the word 'why'. Be sure to support your explanation with evidence.

Extenuating/Exeptional Circumstances Form (ECF)   This is what universities use to recognise and record students' reasons for not being able to complete assessments. universities will have a policy about what is permissible. For example, if you are unable to continue due to medical reasons or a bereavement.

External examiner (External verifier/External moderator)   A third party academic from a different university who will check a run of marks and assessments to ensure that the assessment process has been fair and that assessment procedures are rigorous.

Familiarisation (practice/mock) test   These tests could be issued by your lecturer or you could find one yourself and it is used to help you practise in preparation for your real assessment.

Fill-in-the-blank assessment type   As the name suggests, in these assessments you have gaps in sentences that you have to complete with the correct words/phrases. This might be an exercise that is then submitted as part of your learning journal.

Formative   This is a piece of assessed work during your learning journey that will help you to continue forming your ideas and understanding of a subject.

Internal modifier (IM) (Internal verifier/Second marker)   This is a member of the academic team within the department you are studying under who will check a run of marks and assessments to ensure fair practice. They will raise concerns with the first marker if they think the original mark is too high or too low. You might not receive back your marks until it has gone through this process so that marks are validated first.

Likert scale questioning   These are often used in surveys where the respondent is asked to strongly agree, agree, neither agree or disagree, disagree or strongly disagree, for example. This then allows the researcher to measure responses from all respondents to get a fixed measurement.

Marks   These are the points awarded to the candidate for each answer given. The maximum number of marks per question will be noted by the questions generally.

Moderation   This is the assessment process by which assessment marks are ratified.

Multiple-choice question   These questions offer you a selection of answers and you must try to select the correct one(s).

Plagiarism   This means presenting someone else's work or ideas as your own and is not acceptable at any level of academic study.

Platform (online)   This is the user interface of a website or online service. This term includes Virtual Learning Environments (VLEs), video conferencing websites and so on.

Portal   This is a password-protected gateway into a website.

Portfolio   This is a collection of work to be submitted for a summative assessment usually. It is often used in vocational courses or the arts as an assessment method.

Proof-reading   Checking through your work for any errors in spelling, grammar and facts.

References   You must acknowledge your sources if you directly quote from them. Check the style or referencing guide from your department to be sure that you have referenced correctly.

Short-answer question   This requires only a short answer such as a short phrase or a few sentences.

Source material   These are files that will be given to you for your assessment to allow you to use them when formulating your answers. You may be able to interact with the material, highlighting online or editing the information.

Summative   A summative assessment is the sum of your learning and the marks from this will be recorded and considered to establish your overall grade.

Technology Enhanced Learning (TEL)   There is a team in your university that is responsible for the technology that academics and students use for learning and assessment. Generally, it is academics who seek out their assistance. However, you might be signposted to a TEL member of staff if you need technical support.

Upload   Once you have a document that you are happy with and want to share, you would upload it, which is to say that you would send/save a copy to an online platform or send it via email to your intended recipient.

Virtual Learning Environment (VLE)   Each university will have its own version of a VLE, which is a place where resources, course information and contact details are shared. It is also a place for video conferencing with online seminars and lectures being delivered through this.

Resources

For further information about online assessments, you could look at your institution's website as we have found that universities have a wealth of information to help you prepare for online assessments. You could also look at the Super Quick Skills series produced by Sage for some inspiration. Here is a list of some of the titles that will be of particular interest to you:

Anderson, L. and Spark, G. (2020) *Pass Your Exam.* London: Sage
Becker, L. (2019) *Give Great Presentations.* London: Sage
Coleman, H. (2019) *Polish Your Academic Writing.* London: Sage
Lancaster, T. (2019) *Avoid Plagiarism.* London: Sage
Leicester, M. and Taylor, D. (2019) *Take Great Notes.* London: Sage
Rabel, K. (2020) *Manage Your Time.* London: Sage
Salmons, J. (2020) *Your Super Quick Guide to Learning Online.* London: Sage
Shon, P.C. (2019) *Cite Your Source.* London: Sage
Shon, P.C. (2019) *Plan Your Essay.* London: Sage
Wilson, C. (2019) *Manage Your Stress*. London: Sage

There are many websites that you might look to for help with your online assessment. Here is one that you will find useful for making practice quizzes:

Create a Revision Resource – Quizzes (getrevising.co.uk/make/quizzes)

The following website covers reflection and learning styles amongst other subjects that you might find useful:

www.sussex.ac.uk/skillshub/?id=476

Index

CPSIA information can be obtained
at www.ICGtesting.com
Printed in the USA
JSHW071412020423
39733JS00002B/57